THE MYSTERY
OF THE KADDISH

THE MYSTERY
OF THE
KADDISH

Its Profound Influence on Judaism

LEON H. CHARNEY
AND
SAUL MAYZLISH

BARRICADE BOOKS
FORT LEE, NEW JERSEY

Published by Barricade Books Inc.
185 Bridge Plaza North
Suite 308-A
Fort Lee, NJ 07024

www.barricadebooks.com

ISBN 1-56980-300-5

First Printing

CONTENTS

DEDICATIONS

*T*HIS BOOK COULD not have seen the light of day without the close and meticulous scrutiny and observations of Professor Nathaniel Laor, a cohort and companion of mine who exemplifies and represents friendship in its truest and greatest sense. Even these words underestimate and undervalue a unique friendship. A renowned psychiatrist, philosopher, and poet and in my opinion, one of the keenest Jewish historical and Talmudic minds. This book owes him immeasurable gratitude and for that I am forever grateful.

To my publisher, Lyle Stuart who I owe enormous debt for personally undertaking the job of super editor. Stuart, an icon in the publishing business, certainly added immense readability to the contents of this book.

To Allan Wilson, my editor, who with his polite mannerisms, has always had a keen eye for the readable and understandable.

To Dr. Charles Friedlander, a renowned physician who represents the closest of friendship and is a true intellectual buddy who was a constant inspiration and kept pushing me to keep going when I thought I was stalled.

To Mark Jaffe, a luminous editor who assisted at the beginning of this project to formulate an outline.

To my office staff:

To my former personal assistant, Sharon Hart-Wagner, always available, always professional and loyal, who unfortunately had to relocate in the middle of this project.

To Bruce Block, talented and exceptionally capable colleague, who is always considerate and helpful of my time and energies. To Rob Essex who always gives me his absolute loyalty and an oasis of time so that I can fulfill my writing periods while he takes care of my business matters. To Nikki Istrefovic who is always dutiful, loyal, and helpful. To Darrell Paster, always available to assist.

To Paula Griffiths who assisted with administrative details.

To Ivy McFadden, for her alacrity and wisdom in helping with editorial changes.

To Edna Lavie who helped us enormously with the Hebrew script.

And finally to Judaism that inspired me to challenge and study.

This book is dedicated to the blessed memory of my parents,
Morris (Shmuel Moshe) and Sara, and my brother, Herb (Chaim).
May their lives be blessed forever. Zichronam li'vracha.

LHC

PREFACE

*I*T STARTED AS a curiosity. My mother died and I was confronted by the question of how and when to say the Mourner's *Kaddish*. Despite my Jewish education, I became aware that I knew little about the origin of the mystical prayer for the dead.

At this point, I questioned some rabbis and scholars regarding the authorship of *Kaddish*. To my surprise they had many hypotheses but few concrete answers.

Here was a universally respected Jewish prayer—one deeply moving and relevant to all Jews—yet it was hard to detect its historical roots.

Intellectually curious, I wondered how could this be? Why such a deep mystery? My circle of friends and acquaintances—men and women, religious and secular—were all ready and willing to recite this prayer after the death of a loved one, yet no one could reliably pinpoint its source.

I decided to try to find answers. In the course of the quest that followed, I discovered that the *Kaddish* prayer reflected and illuminated much of the history of the Jewish people in the Middle Ages. In addition, I found that its origin was quite surprising because of its trans-cultural aspects.

This book will show that the tragedies that beset the Jews in the Middle Ages compelled the rabbis to look to Christians for a means to create a ritual that would help Jews to ventilate their mourning, grief, and sorrow. This is referred to as *hukkot ha'goyim* (the laws of the gentiles). The practice of borrowing ritual from non-Jews is generally forbidden by Jewish biblical and halachic law.

The chapters that follow will show how the rabbis incorporated some of these rituals into the *Kaddish*, or prayer for the dead. They will show directly and indirectly how Jewish folklore and wisdom were applied spiritually, psychologically, and socially to sustain the prayer under unusually complicated and often disastrous circumstances.

It is often said that if you have three Jews in a community, you will have four synagogues and probably many more rabbinical interpreters. This is a kind of metaphor for the fact that Jews and Judaism produced and produces enormous amounts of authoritative knowledge, debates, commentary, interpretations, prayers, and rituals on how the practice of the religion should be upheld or applied.

Judaism has an enormous reservoir of knowledge and

different branches (Orthodox, Conservative, and Reformed), and there are multifarious opinions in all of these branches and on every subject. This discourse on any Jewish subject is humongous and fills volume upon volume.

I started this voyage to try to get a clearer picture of the prayer for the recitation of the Orphan's *Kaddish*. When I thought about writing this book, I understood that I was undertaking to write a book about *Kaddish*, one of the most renowned prayers in Judaism, and it would invite possible controversy and surely comments and conversation. These are all welcome by the author.

This book has given me much more understanding of the impact of *Kaddish* in general and the Orphan's *Kaddish*, and by writing it, my wish is to relay the fascinating information and history that I found with the possibility of enlightening others. The revelations in this book are my personal subjective voyage incorporating ideas which, while authorities may differ, will hopefully illuminate the reader and encourage his or her own curiosity about such a meaningful prayer and its raison d'être.

The book is my understanding, along with that of Saul Mayzlish, of the history and evolution of the *Kaddish* prayer. However, in no way is this interpretation meant to be the only one. Perhaps others who make a similar study might arrive at different conclusions. After all, a spiritual river has many different tributaries and only an individual with extreme hubris would believe that his or her path is the only waterway for the truth.

Leon H. Charney
New York, New York

PROLOGUE

$\mathcal{W}$ E MET AT the Hilton Hotel in Tel Aviv after years of separation: Leon Charney and Saul Mayzlish. Mayzlish tells me he thinks of me as a "renaissance man": internationally prominent lawyer, New York businessman, TV moderator, and former U.S. Presidential advisor. I tend to think of myself as just a boy from Bayonne, New Jersey. Mayzlish is a prominent Orthodox Jew who has written many books popularizing Judaism. I have always appreciated his wisdom in print and on radio and television, where he is considered a personality in the religious community.

The sun was setting in the west and my first question was, "Saul, where is the nearest *minyan*? I'm still in the *shloshim* [the first thirty days following the death] of my mother." Saul seemed to be taken aback, having thoughts that my style of life might preclude my dedication to the commitment of saying *Kaddish* for a year. He was wrong.

We walked together to the synagogue nearest the hotel. We arrived just in time for the final moments of the service. We glanced at one another and Mayzlish observed that I seemed transformed as I stood to say *Kaddish*. But why? It was simply a recitation of a familiar prayer, yet it elicited sparks of intense devotion.

And I, best described as a modern traditional Jew, would not miss saying *Kaddish*. And the same applied to the other two daily prayer services as well, day after day, week after week, for a full eleven months. Airplane flights, computers, international business deals, hobnobbing with world leaders—they were all secondary to my need to say *Kaddish* for my mother.

Mayzlish, too, reminded himself of the time he had said *Kaddish* for his mother, some six years earlier. He, too, had felt tremendous pressure to rush to prayers, squeezing time out of an already overcrowded schedule. Not to say *Kaddish* for his mother three times a day was unthinkable. After all, as is written in the Talmud's Tractate *Sotah* 49a, the world exists due to the merit of those who repeat the *Kaddish* refrain: *Yehei sh'mei rabbah*: "May His great name be blessed."

Those three words in Aramaic are the basis of our Jewish religion.

Non-observant Jews—and Gentiles as well—think of *Kaddish* as simply a prayer for the dead. When we see people who ordinarily never set foot into a synagogue and suddenly they are regulars only because a parent has passed away, they're there to recite the *Kaddish*. We think in our heart of hearts that the reason they are coming to pray is because of their parents and their *Avot* (forefathers). It is considerably more than that.

What is the power of this prayer that people rearrange their lives just in order to say it three times daily in the presence of a *minyan,* a quorum of ten adult Jews?

Why is this prayer so potent?

We refer to the holy books, to the rabbis, and to the academicians. From these we find a very wide range of views, traditions, and sources. We discover amazing historical facts and wide variations of the text in different Jewish communities. One might say that you can study the complete Jewish world by examining how this single prayer relates to a community.

Kaddish is recited in Lublin and Prague, in Baltimore and New York, in London and Moscow, in Tripoli and Alaska. It is spoken around the world wherever there is a Jewish community. In most but not all cases, the text is similar. The words penetrate deeply into the emotions of the prayer-sayers.

So why is this prayer so imbedded in Jewish tradition that it is embraced by all Jews, secular or religious?

To find answers we embarked on a voyage to uncover the mystery of the *Kaddish.* The journey took us to many places, physically, virtually, and philosophically. We encountered a multitude of attitudes, customs, opinions, and beliefs. There were different approaches to religious tradition—Chassidic, Orthodox, Conservative, or Reform. In addition, we found many religious practices were trans-cultural. But somehow, no matter the approach, the recitation of *Kaddish* is a touchstone and bedrock.

As the reader will see, the study of the *Kaddish*, is not only an attempt to solve a mystery but a walk in the garden of the history and legal practice of Judaism.

Here it is, translated from the Aramaic text, as I spoke it, that day in Tel Aviv.

Mourner's Kaddish

Exalted and hallowed be His great Name throughout the world, which He has created according to His will.

May He establish His kingship, bring forth His redemption and hasten the coming of His Messiah in your lifetime and in your days and in the lifetime of the entire House of Israel, speedily and soon, and say, Amen.

May His great Name be blessed forever and to all eternity. Blessed and praised, glorified, exalted and extolled, honored, adored and lauded be the Name of the Holy One, blessed be He, beyond all the blessings, hymns, praises and consolations that are uttered in the world; and say, Amen.

May there be abundant peace from Heaven, and a good life for us and for all Israel; and say, Amen.

He who makes peace in His heavens, may He make peace for us and for all Israel; and say, Amen.

Here, then, the search begins.

PART ONE

Kaddish as a Stalwart of Judaism

In the following chapters we explore how one of the most integral prayers of the Jewish people is practiced in different communities and cultures under various rabbinical interpretations. Additionally, we see how its recitation is reflected in those communities while integrating some of the culture that exists under its sovereignty.

We examine the musical and tonal complexities of the recitation of the Kaddish and the implications of this on its meaning. The familial obligation to recite the Kaddish is discussed and how this works to engage diverse practitioners in the mourning process. Finally, we look at the historical beginnings of the Kaddish and brutal world events that led to its induction into Jewish law.

The history of the Kaddish is a rich and complex one, filled with nuance and a blend of explanations and meanings. As one comes to the point of approaching this prayer it becomes a pivotal vehicle for Jews of any and all sects to connect with their Jewish faith.

· 1 ·

A First Appraisal

*K*ADDISH IS PRIMARILY a prayer of praise and homage to God. It appeals to God to reveal and enhance His honor among all who worship him. It is a prayer to increase faith in God throughout the world.

It was believed that when a person dies, it is as if God has deducted something of his own creation and the Kaddish recited by another human being, son or otherwise, will fill up the empty space.

The original text of the *Kaddish* does not appear in any of our sources as a single answer to our questions. Instead, it is a mosaic of verses and quotes so remarkable, we are told, that when Jews enter their synagogues and prayer halls and pray *Yehei sh'mei rabbah mevorach*,[1] the Holy One sits and nods, saying, "Fortunate is the King who is praised in his home" (Talmud, *Berach* 3a).

The *Kaddish* is recited ten times a day, since it is included in the three public prayers of the day: *Shacharit, Min'cha*, and *Arvit*. The daily prayers are believed to have been created by the three Fathers (*Avot*) of the Nation (Abraham, Isaac, and Jacob) respectively. The ten recitals of the *Kaddish* correspond directly to the Ten Commandments, which are the bedrock of Jewish life. The *Kaddish* prayer is valid only when said in the presence of a *minyan* (ten men in the Orthodox community and egalitarian in Conservative or Reform Judaism). Thus, the *Kaddish* prayer is integrated under the Ten Commandments and thus Congregational Judaism.

Another explanation of the obligation to pray three times daily is that the prayers replace the worship at the Temple where public sacrifices were carried out morning and evening while private sacrifices were done during the day.

At first the prayer was apparently an individual one and had no rigid composition. The Levitical singing has gradually become a public prayer and was established as such after the destruction of the Temple. Daniel in the Book of Daniel was the first individual mentioned in the Bible to pray three times a day (ch. 55:17–18).

Kaddish is written in Aramaic, a close relative of Hebrew and the language spoken by the Jewish people at the time it was composed.[2] The Haggadah-homiletic literature notes that this prayer is so important that even the angels, who praise God constantly, would be jealous of its recitation, had they but known its content. However, we are told that the angels did not understand Aramaic and thus did not envy us.

The angels, who are not faced with each person's daily struggle for survival to earn a living, to feel secure, and to face the world's many challenges, cannot fathom that which the mortals can. How poignant these words are and how they resonate with us. What can the angels in heaven know about us in our vibrant modern world? What can they know about the State of Israel where lives are in constant danger from wars in the past and terrorists in the present, a genuine existential battle? The angels know nothing of this.

People know. People feel empathy for the words of the *Kaddish* even if they have no knowledge of the language itself. There is no rational explanation for how it has become one of the important measures by which one Jew relates to another.

The late Ezer Weizman, the esteemed former head of the Israeli Air Force and President of Israel, once assessed my role in the secret and delicate talks between Egypt and Israel. "Leon Charney," said Weizman to Mark Segal, a reporter for the *Jerusalem Post*, "is the most Jewish American I have met. I remember that when we were in Atlanta, he awakened me at six in the morning on a rainy day to accompany him to the synagogue so that he could say *Kaddish* for his father.

"Charney offered me a different point of view from which to see things. I was drawn to him because I am still influenced by my father's father, to whom I only spoke Yiddish. I did not receive a religious education because, in my family, Zionism meant a total break with Eastern Europe. We disdained the *golah*—the Diaspora—but not Judaism. This explains why I identified with him from our very first meeting."

The first port of call on our journey was a small Chassidic *shtibl* (literally a "little house")—the term used for small synagogues of the type common in the Eastern European *shtetl* (a term used to connote a small village). The one we chose was located in the center of Tel Aviv, on Nordau Street. It had been used for decades by Gur Chassidim who came to Israel after World War II and the Holocaust. Its establishment followed the pattern set in Eastern Europe.

In earlier times, each town or village had a single central synagogue. However, as the towns became larger, the single synagogue often didn't accommodate the growing Jewish population. In addition, the central synagogue was sometimes far from the homes of many of the Jews. The *shtiblach* (plural of *shtibl*) were thus built as small secondary synagogues, as needed or desired by the people of a certain location or with a common way of life.

There was even an historical precedent. The Talmud (*Ketubot* 105a) tells us that at the time of the destruction of the Temple in 70 C.E., there were hundreds of synagogues in Jerusalem, each one serving a different locality or "guild." For example, there were synagogues for leather workers, shoemakers, tailors, butchers, etc.

This arrangement continued through the centuries. It is told, for example, that the saintly Chafetz Chaim of Radin[3] would make the rounds of all the different "occupational" synagogues, where he would lecture—with a single exception. He would never enter the synagogue of the teachers. When asked why, he explained that in each of these "occupational" synagogues there were inherent dangers: At the synagogue of the glaziers there might be glass on the floor, at that of the shoemakers there could be nails. But in the synagogue of the teachers he was afraid that he might be stepping on bits and pieces of the souls of the students, because that was their "stock in trade."

In the Kehal Chassidim synagogue in Tel Aviv there was a lack of formality, a common trait among all Chassidic *shtiblach*. There is a clear lack of order, books lie around haphazardly, and there is a rather flexible adherence to announced prayer times. On the other hand, the prayers are recited with real devotion and there is closeness among the "regulars." One feels that it is almost like a single family.

When we prayed there during the *Shacharit* (daily Jewish morning prayer), men came to us from time to time to adjust our tefillin, for the tefillin box worn on the head must be centered. Glances were cast at us because of our modern, relatively colorful clothing (the vast majority of congregants in this *shtibl* limit the colors of their clothing to black and white). And it was only with difficulty that the ten males needed for a *minyan* were assembled, as most of the Chassidim who lived in the area had moved to Chassidic neighborhoods or towns.

In this *shtibl* the members do not restrict themselves only to communal prayers and Torah study. This is also a major social gathering place, and each person has a great deal of freedom to express himself. No morning prayer there is complete without what is called *tzav*—the Hebrew word for a "directive." To partake of *tzav*, as they see it, is a religious requirement.

What is *tzav*? It is a Hebrew term which means literally "to command." If we apply the Hebrew system of *gimatria*, each Hebrew letter has a numerical equivalent, which creates a multitude of different meanings. The word is composed of the letters *tzaddi* with a numerical value of 90, and *vav*, with a value of 6, or together 96. This means, you are told, that you must have a shot of "96"—a drink that is 96 percent alcohol (192 proof!), as close to pure alcohol as one can get. Accordingly, if one drinks a glass of "96," it cleans the slate of all one's sins of the past 24 hours. If one happens to sin during the day, the next day's "96" will serve to atone for that day's sins. Thus, every day one can start anew with a clean slate.

We asked the oldest congregant, Rabbi Yaakov Cohen, one of the veteran Gur Chassidim, for his knowledge of the origin of the *Kaddish*. Even though it was a regular workday, Cohen, who had just finished his term as prayer leader, agreed to spend time with us if it would help.

He began our discussion by repeating the prayer. But he did something different: He incorporated a melody in an effort to add meaning to his words. Using a unique melody when this prayer is recited could very well be in the Chassidic tradition that everything in the world, no matter how commonplace or prosaic, has a spark of the Divine in it, which a melody helps both heighten and illustrate. "You are correct," said the rabbi, "that within the melody sung by people to recite the *Kaddish*, one senses a yearning for the source of all good in the world, That is the Holy One, Blessed be He."

The rabbi continued, "Let us start with history. You know that the *Kaddish* is recited in Aramaic. The important thing is that it should be understood. The prayer itself was written when the Jews were in Babylon. Since most people at that time spoke very little Hebrew, the prayer was formulated in Aramaic and interwoven with a few Hebrew phrases, which they did understand.

"The primary consideration of the wise men was that the people who said it and those who answered the refrain knew exactly what was being said. The different sections were not joined into a single prayer, so fragments remained in Aramaic, which, of course, is closely related to Hebrew. It is the same language, you know, in which some of our greatest works were written, including Talmuds, the Zohar, and several of the books of the Bible."[4]

"Does that mean," we asked, "that the *Kaddish* gradually added various elements along the way?" In typical Chassidic fashion, Cohen began humming a beautiful Yemenite tune before answering. When he finished, he said quietly, "Yes."

"Yes," he repeated, "When Maimonides was alive, the Yemenite Jews added to the *Kaddish* the words, 'and in the life of our master Moses ben Maimon,' the giant of Torah thought, about whom it was said, 'From Moses (the lawgiver) until Moses (ben Maimon) there never arose in Israel another like Moses.'"

The rabbi went on to point out another example of added words found among the famous Genizah fragments from Cairo. This document evidently notes the complete text of a *Kaddish* which was customarily used in eleventh-century Israel relating to the most important rabbis living at that time.

In the opening of the *Kaddish* the familiar phrases are expanded: "*yitgadal ve'itkadash sh'mei rabbah be'alma di vera chirutei yamlich malchutei ve'yatzmach purkanei vi'yakrev meshichei; be'chayei adoneinu Evyatar ha'Kohen rosh yeshivat ga'on ya'akov u've'chayei rabbenu Shelomo ha'Kohen av ha'yeshivah u've'chayei rabbenu Tzadok, ha-shelishi she'ba'-havurah, u've'hayyekhon.*"

The translation of this is: Magnified and sanctified be His great Name in the world which He has created according to His will. May He establish His kingdom during the life of our master Evyatar ha-Cohen, the head of the Yeshivah Gaon Ya'akov, and during the life of Solomon ha-Cohen, principal of the yeshiva, and during the life of our Rabbi Zadok, the third member of the heads, and during your life.

Cohen was obviously deep in thought. Then he said, "You know, for centuries we haven't added words to the *Kaddish*, except for the slight changes included during the Ten Days of Repentance. Nor have we dropped any words in all that time. And during the Ten Days, when we add the word *le'eilah*, we make sure to change *min kol* to *mikol*,[5] to make certain that the number of words in the *Kaddish* remain the same."

He added: "Nowadays, in general, the language of the *Kaddish* is very similar among the different groups of Jews. Within the same group there may be variations, but these are of a minor nature."

We interrupted: "But when was the *Kaddish* finally formulated into a unit? When, in essence, was a single standard core component established, to which various elements were added over time?"

Cohen did not give us a direct answer. Instead, he noted that the short version of the Kaddish, generally referred to as *chatzi Kaddish*—the "Half *Kaddish*"[6]—is spoken at various times during the communal prayers as a prelude to certain sections of the prayers and after the reading of the Torah. This basic *Kaddish* was then extended to form the *Kaddish titkabel*, often known as the "Whole *Kaddish*." This is recited at the end of the major part of each of the daily prayers (as Cohen pointed): "It is a request by us of God to accept our prayers, and asks that Jews be brought together in peace with one another."

That same *Kaddish*, minus the one sentence which asks God to accept the prayers of the congregation, is the famous *Kaddish yatom*—the "Mourner's *Kaddish*." The *Kaddish yatom* is added to each of the daily prayers and after the chapters of the Psalms in a *minyan*. It is generally said by mourners during the time they are in mourning and on the *yahrzeit* of the death of a close relative.

Rabbi Cohen then began to discourse about the *Kaddish d'rabbanan*[7]—the "Rabbis' *Kaddish*"—and the *Kaddish hagadol*—the "Great *Kaddish.*" At this point he was really out of time and we promised to return to hear the rest of his learned views on the subject.

Now we hastened to a meeting with one of the most sought-after lecturers in the field of Jewish thought. Coincidentally, he was yet another Cohen, Dr. Yuval Cohen. We wanted to ask him too about the establishment of the *Kaddish* as the basic prayer recited by mourners.

Yuval Cohen seemed clearly a person who has lived with prayers most of his life. He is a distinguished Talmud scholar, yet one trained in the scientific disciplines; he is young, buoyant, full of the joy of being, yet rooted firmly in the Jewish world of prayer.

Dr. Cohen began by telling us that the link between the *Kaddish* and the prayer for the dead is not mentioned anywhere in the ancient sources, neither in the Talmud nor in the oldest *midrashim*, the enormous fount of traditional stories explicating the Hebrew Bible.

Yes, there are references to the need to pray for a departed father, so that he may find eternal rest in the "world that is purely good." This point is addressed specifically in Tractate *Kallah*[8] a section of the Talmud edited at the time of the *Geonim*. This was long after the early Talmudic era.

This reference, though, still does not mention saying *Kaddish* for departing relatives as a custom.

At this point, it was I who introduced a concept that I had come across in reading some years earlier (in fact, while I was sitting *shivah* after my mother's death, often also a time of study and meditation). This concept, set out by Ivan Marcus in David Biale's *Culture of the Jews: A New History*,[9] proposes that *Kaddish* became a mourning prayer as a response to the violence committed against the Jews during the Crusades and thereafter, during the 11th to the 13th centuries.

Professor Cohen, was resistant to this idea in our initial conversation. Later he came to embrace it and this inspired him to provide further insights as we explored with him the general social, national, and historical aspects of our search.

The basic question then was what is the Mourner's *Kaddish* and why is it a prayer for the dead when it actually makes no mention of the termination of life or of death itself? Is it meant to be an internalization of the acceptance of God's decree? Is it an attempt to understand why a person who was so beloved was taken from his family and his friends? Is it meant to explain why that person was taken away forever?

Does the *Kaddish* come to terms with the feelings of pain, anger, and depression which envelop survivors after such a loss? There are sound, historical reasons why questions, which every mourner asks about the deaths of his loved ones, must be answered in the context of a developing liturgy.

Such questions were asked even more poignantly at the time the *Kaddish* was made an obligation for mourners, for it was the time of the Crusades. This was a period when countless Jews were massacred, especially in Germany. In retrospect, it foreshadowed the Nazis, for in ancient Germany, Jews were told, "You can't work here. Nor can you attend our schools." Then: "You can't live here." And finally, with Hitler, "You can't live."

Nor was the murder of Jews confined to within German

borders. It was often free time for Jew-hunting in neighboring nations. Also, it was the time of the Plague and the Black Death. These killers didn't discriminate and gentiles by the millions suffered early and painful death along with the Jews.

The Jews, who were suffering constant persecution, had developed a sort of immunity to it. Suffering the slings and arrows of Jew-hating and Jew-baiting and Jew-killing, they licked their wounds after the Crusaders' legions had marched away.

Then they found a way to express their grief. For example, Rabbi Elazar ben Natan, one of the first *Tosafots*, composed all of the kinot[10]—memorial dirges—that are recited on a fast day memorializing or mourning the destruction of the Jewish temples. These were in memory of the Crusade of 1096, in which he described how entire Jewish communities on the Rhine had been slaughtered. These kinot also incorporate prayers. Again, in 1146, there were pogroms against the Jews, with the active encouragement from the clergy. Then, in 1282, in Spires, the first blood libel trial was held and Jews were burned alive at the stake.

In 1349, the Jewish communities of Spires, Worms, and Magence were destroyed. Jews were killed, forcibly converted, or forced to flee for their lives. All of this was the result of accusations that it was they who had caused the Black Death. This terrible plague that spread throughout Europe in the 14th century and killed no fewer than 25 million people, vanished as mysteriously as it had arrived.

After the plague subsided, the entire continent of Europe was in despair. This was coupled with feelings of guilt, as people believed that it was their own sinning which had brought the plague. As a result, there was a tendency toward asceticism and toward separating the "outsider" from the rest of humanity. The plague was regarded as a heavenly punishment for the evils of the world. Groups of penitents sought to mortify their flesh, wandering from city to city, preaching the need for repentance—and, as a sideline, instigating pogroms against the Jews.

Among the masses, rumors spread—or were spread deliberately—that the Black Plague had indeed been caused by the Jewish outsiders and that those strangers with their strange ways had poisoned the wells in order to destroy the Christian world.

When the Plague hit Chillon in Savoy (today's Switzerland) all the Jews were arrested. One of them "confessed" under torture that a group of Jews in southern France had prepared a white powder made of the hearts of Christians, spiders, frogs, lizards, human flesh, and the Host wafers used in the Catholic Mass. This powder, it was claimed, was delivered to special Jewish agents who used it to poison the Christian wells and cause the Plague.

Accusations were repeated throughout the region and the Rhineland. They soon spread to other parts of Germany, often along with a repetition of the "blood libel." In Zurich, a number of Jews were burned alive, while the rest were expelled. In Augsburg, in Wurzburg, and in all the towns of Bavaria, there were riots against the Jews. In Freiburg, every known Jew was killed except for 12 wealthy men who delayed their ultimate fate by bribing the authorities. In Spires, some members of the Jewish community were killed, some chose to commit suicide, and some saved themselves by converting to Catholicism.

The mayor of Strasbourg refused to believe that the Jews

had caused the plague. He was removed from his office and 2,000 Jews were burned to death on an island in the Rhine just outside of the city. In Worms, 400 Jews were burned to death.

The Jews of Frankfurt perished in a fire in their ghetto which they themselves had set. The fire spread to other parts of the city. In Meinz, the Jews organized a defense force and killed 200 of those who attacked them, but when they realized they could no longer hold out, they burned themselves to death along with all their possessions.[11]

We are told that 6,000 Jews died in Magence on August 22, 1349 (the poem by Saul Tchernichowsky, on "Baruch of Magenza," refers to that incident). In Cologne, 3,000 Jews died violent deaths at the hands of the mob. By the end of 1349, 300 Jewish communities had been attacked.

The Jews of Germany were almost wiped out, and the few survivors lived in constant fear. They prayed, as we do today, asking God to "remove from us all enemies, plague, the sword, hunger, and suffering." Their prayers received no answer.

By the end of the 14th century the persecutions of previous centuries created among the Jews the need for a special prayer. It would be said for those parents, children, and the masses of co-religionists who had been killed while sanctifying God's name. Speculation is that the need was caused by the fact that their gentile neighbors, who had also been affected by the plague, had special prayers for mourning and suffering, and the Jews needed their own versions of such prayers.

The *Kaddish* prayer suited their need in reacting to the attacks of the mobs against them. A number of prayers and kinot were composed at the time to commemorate this terrible era. For example, the *Av Harachamim* prayer, said on

Sabbath mornings, calls upon God to revenge the blood of the innocents.

The tradition of reciting the *yizkor* prayer in memory of the departed also traces back to that time. It would appear, though, that the biggest change was the use of the *Kaddish* prayer by those who survived the religious fanaticism of the Christian world during the Crusades. The bottom line was that multitude of all the Jews of Germany (and of the Holy Land as well[12]) had been murdered by the Christians.

Let us turn to the text itself. The *Kaddish* seems at the beginning, to be huge, abstract, and threatening. It increases the greatness of God, but only later does it become positive in its approach to God. In mediaeval times, the contradiction appears. How can one say that God is excellent and sing a song of glory to Him, while Jews die by the thousands? This question has survived to our own time, the time of the Holocaust, when Jews died by the millions.

The big question of holy justice remains: where was God in Auschwitz?

It remains unanswered and has shaken the faith of many, converting thousands of Jews into non-believing atheists.

There is the story of two concentration camp survivors who were traveling on the same train. In the morning, one of them took out his tefillin and offered them to his friend. The latter refused them. Then he suggested breakfast to his friend and again the latter refused. At noon time suddenly the friend took out his own tefillin and put them on, and then he took out his breakfast and began eating.

"Why did you refuse my offer?" said the first man.

Said his friend, "As a survivor of the Holocaust I have a soul searching for God; I searched for him till the last moment of the command to put on tefillin. Even He must be suffering a little."

Both during the Holocaust and the Middle ages, the suffering of the Jews gave rise to strong nationalist feelings, fanning hopes for redemption and resulted in the formation of a messianic movement and the development of the Kabbalah.[13]

Kaddish filled the needs of mourners because it was the most visible of all Jewish mystical texts. It was also appropriate to say this prayer at any time because it refers to God in the third person. This means there is no question of using God's name in vain.

The *Kaddish* doesn't call on the sacred name of God but instead uses appellations such as "the Holy One, Blessed be He." Thus, the first line speaks about "His great Name" without any further elaboration. Just as a person at times of crisis and calamity needs a support mechanism, the *Kaddish*, by the very act of addressing God, offers the prayer-sayer support in his time of need. Just as at the end of any public Torah reading, the *Kaddish* is appropriate, with its reference to messianic times and its message of comfort. The same applies when it is said by a single person in distress, or even by the nation as a whole.[14]

This natural way of addressing God, with the acceptance of what has happened and the implicit messianic vision therein, includes special hope for the revival of the dead. That, of course, was particularly appropriate for those communities affected by the Crusades and the "Black Death."

A story told by the great sage Rabbi Akiva, tells of a man sentenced to *Gehinom* who was saved from it by the fact that he had taught his son to say *Kaddish*. Such a tale offered hope to the unfortunate Jews of Europe, and this story remained part of the communal memory for generations. Thus, even the Jews of Germany under the heel of their Nazi persecutors, found in *Kaddish* a text that comforted and calmed them. Always too was hope that the bad times would pass and be replaced by a better future.

The *Kaddish* declares that we must accept the verdict from on high and subject ourselves to the Kingdom of Heaven. One must thank God for the bad just as one thanks God for the good. It is legitimate to mourn, and the experience of mourning need not undermine our belief or faith as was espoused by the famous religious philosopher Martin Buber's "I–Thou" relationship with God.[15]

The death of a loved one leaves a void in God's entire universe. Each individual is part of the whole, and therefore every death leaves a vacuum which needs to be filled. How can this be done?

The English poet John Donne expressed it beautifully when he wrote in the middle of the 17th century: "No man is an island, entire of itself; every man is a piece of the continent, a part of the main. If a clod be washed away by the sea, Europe is the less, as well as if a promontory were, as well as if a manor of thy friend's or of thine own were: any man's death diminishes me, because I am involved in mankind, and therefore never send to know for whom the bell tolls; it tolls for thee."

When relatives of the departed recite *Kaddish*, they proclaim God's reign of the universe, praise Him, ask that His name might be revealed and that He make His reign apparent to all. One must accept the fact that He choreographs the world as He sees fit. These elements are all contained in the *Kaddish*. By reciting it, one proclaims God as the Supreme Moral Authority, the One and the Only.

The person who recites the *Kaddish*, fills the vacuum left by the death of the loved one. The rupture is thus healed: Everything that the Holy One does is for the good, whether or not we can understand it.

Another source declares *Kaddish* is Kabbalistic. The Kabbalah sees the *Kaddish* as a request of God to raise up the soul of the departed, to ultimately bring about the realization of the messianic redemption and the awakening of the dead which will accompany this. In other words, we who are still alive are linked to whatever memories the departed person left here on earth, and our *Kaddish* is designed to enhance that link.

The person who says *Kaddish* declares, by the very act of reciting the words that he acknowledges the spiritual heritage which the departed person—his father, mother, or other relative—left behind in the world. When we say *Kaddish* for a dead person, we ask that the departed should intercede on high not only for us personally, but for the entire Jewish people, that out of the departed's love of the Jewish people, we ask that we should act to defend it.

Thus bereavement serves as a means to defend and protect the entire Jewish People. Those who recite *Kaddish* over a deceased person (especially when it is done by the children of the deceased, who carry that person's very genes) increase the appreciation of that person. Even though the person no longer walks among us, his or her influence and aura will continue to be felt and will influence how the next generation acts.

Add to that the concept that the deceased will intercede in heaven on our behalf, so that we will continue to live in peace and harmony, assisted by that person's heavenly help and thus will this world will become a better and more enlightened place.[16]

The theological background of the *Kaddish* serves to explain its popularity as being identified with mourning (and with orphans), even among many cultural Jews who claim to be atheists or doubters. This is clearly the result of communal influence rather than that of rabbis or other leaders. Ordinary people identified with the contents of the *Kaddish*, have made it part of the universal Jewish heritage.

The fact is that there are assimilated Jews who never observed any Jewish practice, often have had no Jewish education, and have no familiarity with Jewish prayer. Despite this, as death approached, they instructed their children to say *Kaddish* for them.

We offer as a typical example, Dr. Moshe Sneh, a famous Zionist leader and former commander of the *Haganah* (Israel's pre-state army) and in addition a leader of the Israeli Communist Party. Dr. Sneh, a highly educated liberal, and a strong proponent of enlightenment, rationalism, and science, totally rejected the religious world into which he had been born. His faith was the political doctrine called Communism and he had embraced that Communist credo which says that religion is "the opium of the masses." Yet Dr. Sneh instructed his son, a physician and politician (who later became a Minister in a Labor government in Israel), to be sure to say *Kaddish* for him according to all the rules.[17]

Dr. Sneh wrote: "The value in terms of tradition of the saying of *Kaddish* surpasses by far any rejection one might feel toward the verbal content of this prayer. If a person does not accept this short explanation of mine, that is irrelevant to me. I believe that we must be loyal to Jewish tradition, for I see it as the secret of our existence, which preserved us and kept us alive as a nation which is both ancient and young at the same time."

· 2 ·

Forever and to All Eternity

ONE SATURDAY, NOT long after our meeting with Yuval Cohen, we walked from our Tel Aviv hotel to a unique synagogue in the heart of Ben Yehudah Street, Ichud Shivat Tziyon.

This synagogue was founded by German Jews who emigrated to what was then called Palestine in the 1930s. This congregation was joined a decade later by a small number of Jews who had survived the Holocaust and made their way to Israel soon after World War II.

A sense of order and discipline permeates this attractive old house of worship. Even though the congregation has shrunk and the number of regular worshippers is now small, there remain some German-language-oriented old-timers who refer to the street on which the synagogue is located as "Ben Yehudah Strasse."

While attending the regular morning prayer service, we found that no fewer than seven different *Kaddish* prayers were recited. The number seven is found in many Jewish religious contexts, and the fact that seven *Kaddish* prayers were said appeared to us to have mystical significance. "Seven,"[18] after all, is the number of days in the week, the Seven Species with which the Land of Israel is blessed, the Seven Blessings recited at a wedding, the seven Noahide.[19] They are considered part of the community of believers obligating all mankind, the seven *Ushpizin* who traditionally visit one's s*ukkah*—one on each of the seven days of *Sukkot*. Then there are the seven days of Pesach, the seven-branched Menorah that stood in the Temple—and now, recited daily in this synagogue, the seven different *Kaddish* prayers.

At the *minchah* (afternoon) and *ma'ariv* (evening) services, there are three or four *Kaddish* prayers, all of which are an integral part of the liturgy. Therefore, even if there are no mourners obligated to recite the *Kaddish yatom*, it is recited by a congregant present at the end of the service. Parenthetically, we may also note that during weekdays, whoever has an obligation to recite the Kaddish *yatom* also has the right to be the *chazan* (cantor) at that prayer. He may not want to act as the *chazan*, and he has the right of "first refusal."

Continuing our inquiry, I asked if there was a standard musical tradition regarding the *Kaddish*.[20] As an amateur *chazan*, it was a natural for me to ask this. Saul, our host at Shivat Tziyon, quoted passages from a popular work by Akiva Zimmerman, the undisputed authority on *chazanut*, regarding the musical traditions of the prayers. According to

Zimmerman, among Ashkenazi Jews the test of an expert *chazan* is the ability to differentiate between the different *Kaddish* melodies for various occasions, and to use the correct melody at the correct time.

Each *Kaddish* melody is unique to its own version of the prayer—with one exception: on *Simchat Torah*, when there is much festivity and frivolity, the *hazan* can combine as many of the *Kaddish* melodies as he wishes. It is known as the *yohr's Kaddish*, or "the annual *Kaddish*." In the hands of a seasoned *chazan*, the *Kaddish* can that day become a total—and often very pleasing—mix of all the melodies used throughout the year. The particular *Kaddish* we heard that morning is used by the Jews whose forbears came from Frankfurt, Germany, and we found touches of other traditions among the worshipers there, most of whom also had family origins in Germany.[21]

Among the worshipers at Ichud Shivat Tziyon were some who noted that as members of congregations, they had instituted several innovations. For example, if a person died leaving only daughters, the women would say *Kaddish* in the presence of ten men. In most other countries, *Kaddish* was an exclusive male domain. The German Jews were scrupulously Orthodox in every other way, but their parents observed their religious tradition with an egalitarian approach to the *minyan*; they realized that it was important to permit a woman who had no brothers to say *Kaddish* for her parents.

Another example: These Jews of German origin insisted that the words *veyatzmach purkanei vikareiv meshichei*, a phrase which is generally recited in those congregations which used the Sephardic prayer customs, should not be added. They wanted to expunge from Judaism messianic overtones relating to the rising of the dead and national redemption, thus maintaining the realistic perspective on death and the human position vis-a-vis "the Divine." At the same time, it is clear that the absence of the words does not detract from an understanding of the central concepts of the *Kaddish*.[22]

After the service we sat down with the congregation's rabbi to take the next step in our search—a step-by-step analysis of the core of the *Kaddish*, that is the "half-*Kaddish*," by referring to the monumental work by Rabbi Adin Steinsaltz, *Ha'Siddur ve'ha'tefillah* (The Siddur and Prayer).[23] It begins with general comments on certain of the Kabbalistic elements involved in the *Kaddish* specifically and in prayers in general.

The *Kaddish* and prayers, he states, may be visualized as a single stairway, something like Jacob's ladder, which reaches down to the ground but whose top reaches the heavens. This reflects man's mission in the world: he needs to have his feet solidly planted on the ground, while his head can soar upward, to the highest peaks of human thought, intellect and imagination. He can only ascend rung by rung. After one reaches the peak, one must of necessity descend to our world. Each prayer chapter parallels a different stage in the development of the soul.

The factor which unites the different elements of the liturgy is the *Kaddish*. At each stage, by means of the *Kaddish*, the person accepts the supremacy of God over all. Thus, *Kaddish* provides us with a mechanism whereby it is possible for us to ascend, a mechanism by means of which we can attain holiness, and then we are forced to descend again to the solid earth of reality. Now that we have returned from this journey through the different stages and worlds, we need the *Kaddish* to reinforce the simple, the natural, and the material aspects of daily life.

This is the text we studied, in a translation that is almost identical in various traditions.

"Glorified and sanctified be God's great name throughout the world which He has created according to His will. May He establish His kingdom in your lifetime and during your days, and within the life of the entire House of Israel, speedily and soon; and say, Amen. May His great name be blessed forever and to all eternity? Blessed and praised, glorified and exalted, extolled and honored, adored and lauded be the name of the Holy One, blessed be He, beyond all the blessings and hymns, praises and consolations that are ever spoken in the world; and say, Amen."

And in the following, more detailed discussion of the *Kaddish*, Rabbi Steinsaltz is our guide, phrase by phrase, the text with references to relevant excerpts from the Torah and other passages from the Bible.

Yitgadal veyitkadash—"Glorified and sanctified be . . ." The main concept underlying the *Kaddish* is to be found in Moses' prayer (Numbers 14:17), "And now, I pray You, let the power of the Lord be great, as You have spoken," which is both a prayer and a request that God's power be magnified and revealed in the world. The two-word combination, *yitgadal veyitkadash*, is based on a verse in Ezekiel 38:23, *vehitgadalti vehitkadashti*—"I will be glorified and sanctified . . . and they will know that I am the Lord."

Shemei rabbah—"[God's] great Name." This is found in I Samuel 12:22, *Shemo hagadol*—The Lord will not forsake

His people for *His great name's sake.*" The word "great" is one of respect and esteem in regard to God's name. However, it also has another meaning, because this phrase is sometimes used for one of the mystical names of God as found in the *Kabbalah*, but not in the Torah. Thus, "His great name" is a reference to God's "true" name, one that no human can comprehend, as opposed to the names we use for God, which are but descriptive names, used by us because of our limited capabilities.

(According to the Founder of Habad Movement Reb Shneur Zalman of Liady in his book "Torah Or" in the Parasha of Vayehy, when we say those words, we are praying to God and begging him that this name should be a Bracha, to bring it down and reveal the hidden light of God that is in the Heavens above, and continue it down. Lealam ulealmey Olmaya, in the worlds below, until the lowest one, our materialistic world. That it shouldn't be just another habit but something that we understand in our brain and feel in our heart.)

Be'al'ma di'vra chirutei—"Throughout the world which He has created according to His will." This parallels Psalms 135:6, "Whatever the Lord wished, He did," namely that God created the world as He wanted it to be, and only He rules it and can change it in whichever way He wishes.

B'chay-yeichon uv'yomeichon—"In your lifetime and during your days." We ask that God's name be glorified and sanctified, not in the distant future, but in the lifetime of the worshippers. It is also possible that the reference to "during your days" is meant to imply that we ask for God to bring this about while we are still "in our days"—while we are still capable of living to the fullest, rather than when we are all old and decrepit.

Uv'chay'yei d'chol beit Yisra'el—"and within the life of the entire House of Israel," the assurance that all will live to see God's ultimate redemption of the world.

Ba-a-gala uvizman kariv—"speedily and soon." This is a new request, building upon the previous one. Not only do we ask for redemption at some point in the lifetime of the congregants, in the distant future, but we ask for it to take place very soon (see Psalms 69:18, for example: "Do not hide Your face from Your servant; for I am in distress; answer me speedily").

V'im'ru: Amein—"and say: Amen." There are many places in the Bible where praise of God is followed by "Amen," as, for example, Psalms 106:48, "Blessed be the Lord, the God of Israel, from everlasting even to everlasting, and let all the people say: 'Amen.'" Everyone is asked to say, "Amen," so that all will take part in the prayer. Thus, rather than being the prayer of a single individual, it becomes the prayer signifying the consent of the entire congregation.

Y'hei sh'mei rabba me'vorach …—"May His great name be blessed …" When the congregation answers, "Amen," it also adds, "May His great name be blessed forever and to all eternity." Some people also add the next word of the *Kaddish* as well: **yitbarach**—"may He be blessed." This phraseology is similar to that in Daniel 2:20, "Daniel spoke and said: 'Blessed be the name of God forever and to all eternity.'"

L'olam ul'ol'mei olma-ya—"forever and to all eternity." The literal translation of this passage is "from one world to the other world." This is similar to I Chronicles 29:10, "for ever and ever" (literally, "from one world to the other world"). The double use of "world" implies both this world and the World to Come, the world in which we live and the World on High.

Yitbarach v'yishtabach ...—"Blessed and praised...." The underlying idea of this sentence is to be found in the verse (Nehemiah 9:5), "Let them say: 'Blessed be your glorious Name that is exalted above all blessing and praise.'" The eight Hebrew words here, from **Yishtabach** through **Veyit'gadal**, though different, are similar in meaning. They deal with exalting God—**v'yitromam v'yitnasei, v'yit-hadar**—"exalted, extolled, and honored," and with glorifying Him—**v'yitpa-ar ... v'yit-hadar**—"glorified ... extolled." Some commentators concerned with the significance of numerical parallels note that if we add to these eight words the first two words of the *Kaddish*, **Yitgadal veyitkadash**—"Glorified and sanctified"—the ten words are the counterparts of the ten "utterances" whereby God created the world, or of the Ten Commandments.

L'ei-la min kol birchata v'shirata ...—"beyond all the blessings and hymns...." We find this idea in Nehemiah 9:5, "Exalted above all blessing and praise. . . ." As Ibn Ezra explains it, "No creature can possible praise Him or exalt Him in accordance with His greatness and elevation, for He is greater and more exalted, to the extent that no mouth can express it."

What that passage in the *Kaddish* tells us is that God is so great and exalted that we cannot even begin to fathom His greatness, and that as much as we praise Him, we have not begun to comprehend how great He is.

Even the Prophets could not begin to fathom His greatness. Thus also in Isaiah 64:3, "Neither has the eye seen a God beside You." This portion of the *Kaddish* concludes with the words, **da-amiran b'al'ma**—"that are ever spoken in the world."—We humbly acknowledge that we can only express

God's greatness in words we can understand, but that our words cannot begin to express God's real greatness; nor can we visualize what the World to Come will be.

Birchata v'shirata, tushb'chata v'ne-che-mata— "blessings and hymns, praises and consolations." According to Kabbalah, each one of these four words is linked to one of the four letters of God's ineffable name, and thus each has special significance.

In most prayer versions, the phrase **L'ei-la min kol**— "beyond all"—is replaced by **L'ei-la (u)le'eila mikol**— "beyond and beyond all"—throughout the Ten Days of Repentance, because during that time God's Divine Presence is more apparent in the world, and He is even more exalted than the rest of the year.

Some prayer versions only make that change in language during the *ne'ilah* prayer, the last prayer of *Yom Kippur*, and the high point of the most solemn day of the Hebrew year.

The foregoing is a typical example of the manner in which phrases and even single words in basic liturgical texts are analyzed and supported. And armed with this new understanding, we moved on to the next phase of our search, which took us, in fact, to the *Hechal Shlomo*, the Great Synagogue, in Jerusalem.

· 3 ·

KADDISH MELODIES

*U*P TO THIS point, we had paid little attention to the varied ways in which *Kaddish* is chanted or sung. But now it was time to study the music of the prayer, and we were advised to pay a visit to Eli Jaffe, one of the major pillars of Jewish music and cantorial expertise.

We met inside the exquisite walls of the Great Synagogue.

Eli is a conductor, but also a composer known throughout the world both for his classical and Jewish compositions.

Being curious, we asked him about his personal background. Instead of talking about himself, he spoke about his father, Dr. Morris A. Jaffe, who was mainly responsible for the construction of this magnificent building we were standing in.

It is here that the Chief Rabbis of Israel are inaugurated and many large meetings held. It hosts festive prayer services, with a choir accompanying *chazan* Naftali Hershtik, who, with his brother, Haaim Eliezer Hershtik, are world leaders in Jewish song and prayer. Eli talks about his father, "the major," as he was known, in recognition of his military rank in postwar Europe. The elder Jaffe was principally known for his humanitarian work in gathering the remnants of Jews from refugee camps as well as the Jewish children who had been hidden in monasteries and elsewhere. He guided them to rehabilitation.

The interior design of the synagogue is remarkably beautiful, and the acoustics are splendid. They offer a fitting showplace for Jaffe's compelling voice. At our request, he sang different melodies used for the *Kaddish* by various Jewish ethnic groups.

He demonstrated a number of such melodies which are comparable to the familiar Ashkenazi "*Hashem Melech*" melody. The Yemenites, on the other hand, Eli tells us, recite all the prayers together with the *chazan* and the melody is the same in all the Yemenite synagogues. Some of the prayers are recited together by the *chazan* and the congregation, while others are recited responsively. Only the males sing, and their melody is a simple one, without any special trills.[24] Returning to a discussion of the Ashkenazim, Jaffe told us there are no fewer than fourteen different melodies for the *Kaddish*, each for a specific time. He described in some detail the work of the aforementioned Akiva Zimmerman, who had explored various Chassidic practitioners of melodies of the

Kaddish. There were, for example, Shmuel Wigoda and David Koussewitsky, who added another *Kaddish* melody, based on bars of "Yankel the Hoarse", as the earlier *Chazan* Yaakov Gottlieb was known.

Shlomo Zulzer, in his Shirei Tziyon, brings a special melody for the *Kaddish* to be recited on *Yom Kippur Katan* (Minor Yom Kippur, the day before *Rosh Chodesh*, dedicated to atonement) which some observe with special prayers). In his Rinah Utefilah, Louis Lewandowski offers a special *Kaddish* to be recited after the reading of the Torah. Then there was Chazan Uriel Moscowitz of Amsterdam, who told Zimmerman that in Holland, at the *minchah* prayer on Yom Kippur he used the melody of *minchah* before a wedding! For those who don't know this, on the day of his wedding a groom is required to fast and to recite the *vidui*—confession—a prayer generally said on Yom Kippur. By transference, the *Kaddish* melody of minchah on Yom Kippur is used on the *minchah* before the wedding. We were told that Zimmerman was also influenced by Nobel Literature Prize-winner S. Y. Agnon's extraordinarily insightful commentary, helpful to either a professional or a simple lay person. In his "Introduction to *Kaddish*," Agnon says, "The reason why we recite *Kaddish* after the dead is to enhance the power of God, and we do not want to enfeeble ourselves before Him, may He be blessed and sanctified, in the worlds which He created in accordance with His will, And we should not fear for ourselves but rather of the grandeur of His holiness, may it be elevated, and may His kingdom be enhanced and revealed to all, and not, Heaven forbid, be diminished in any way." [25]

Finally, we learned that in the *Kaddish* of the Sephardic communities, the use of the *makam* is commonplace. This is an improvisation of the *chazan*, whereby he expresses his feelings, ideas, and mood at a particular time. His only constraint is that he must remain within the framework of the melodies set by the early *payetanim*, as transmitted throughout the generations. This means that the *chazan* is free to use any melody he wishes, provided that it bears some resemblance to the accepted general melody and structure for a particular prayer.

· 4 ·

THE ETERNAL PRAYER

OUR VISIT TO Hechal Shlomo and Eli Jaffe had given us invaluable knowledge about the music of *Kaddish*, but we had two other important stops before leaving Israel. The first was to the Merkaz Ha'rav (a famous Zionist yeshivah in Jerusalem) and to the famed Rabbi Kook's home on Rabbi Kook Street in Jerusalem, where we spent long hours.

Rabbi Avraham Itzhak Ha'cohen Kook was a figure of historic importance in modern Israel, a foremost Torah authority and the first Ashkenazi Chief Rabbi in pre-Israel Palestine.

And why so much time in these places? It was because, in his extensive writings, in which one finds a blend of poetry and deep philosophical thought, Rabbi Kook often stressed the importance of the *Kaddish* as a universal feature of Judaism. Rabbi Kook believed it an integral part of the holiness of the Jewish people, which is tightly bound with the holiness of Eretz Israel, and will exist forever, in spite of all the threats by outsiders to defame and destroy.

One sentence within the *Kaddish* demanded particular attention. This is the refrain: *Y'hei sh'mei rabba me'vorach l'o-lam ul'ol'mei olma-ya*, "May His great name be blessed forever and to all eternity," which is equivalent to Psalms 113:2, "Blessed be the name of the Lord from this time forth and for ever" or to the words we say after reciting the first verse of the *Shema*, "Blessed be the name of His glorious kingdom forever and ever."[26]

It is said that Rabbi Kook would tremble when he heard the people using the latter refrain, because it is one which was used at the time of the First Temple as a response to blessings and prayers. It would be recited twice a day, at the time of the daily sacrifices, when the priests would recite the verse, *Shema Yisrael*, "Hear O Israel, the Lord is our God, the Lord is One." It was also used traditionally after the Blessings of the Priests and on Yom Kippur during the special service of that day, whenever God's ineffable name was said by the High Priest.

The same response was given when the *Hallel* (a liturgical prayer of praise) was recited; that is when the reader intoned, "Praise, servants of the Lord, praise the name of the Lord." And the response was, "May the name of the Lord be blessed forever and ever." These words were also used by the Jews after the destruction of the Second Temple, when Torah study was forbidden and could only be carried out secretly. Thus, at the end of the prayers or of Torah study they became accustomed to saying, "Blessed be the name of the Lord from this time forth and for ever," or, in its Aramaic version, *Y'hei sh'mei rabba me'vorach l'olam ul'ol'mei olma-ya*, "May His great name be blessed forever and to all eternity."

With so rich a history, it is thus not surprising that Rabbi Kook remained in awe of this ancient expression.

In the yeshiva, we met with Rabbi Yochanan Fried, one of the students of Rabbi Kook's son, Rabbi Tzvi Yehudah Kook, and today one of the heads of the Torah Culture Department of the Ministry of Education of Israel. We talked of the teachings of the elder Kook as well as his son, especially their belief that the temporal revival of the Jewish people would bring a spiritual rejuvenation in its wake.

Such rejuvenation would eliminate all disputes and strife among Jews, and the Jewish people would then flock to their own original culture. This brought us back to the *Kaddish* theme, since in it one acknowledges that everything that happens does so because of God's will and God's total supervision over the world.

We were then introduced to one of the young students in the yeshiva, who entered into a lively discussion, in excellent English, of the connection between *Kaddish* and Rabbi Kook's teachings.

As so often happens in Jewish tradition, our new young friend began with a story. Rabbi Moshe of Kobrin once said that if he knew that just one time in his life he had answered *amein* properly, he would never be worried for the rest of his life. In *Seder Hayamim* the sage writes that "if one answers *amein* with all his might, the purification engendered by that cools down the fires of Gehinom for one-and-a-half hours. This prevents the powers of impurity from controlling one's father and mother during those 90 minutes, and brings them to the Garden of Eden."[27]

Our young enthusiast continued his explication, paying special attention to liturgical details. Because of its great importance, in order for a *Kaddish* to be acceptable, he explained that it must be recited in the presence of a quorum. Originally, the rule was that no matter how many mourners were present at the observance, only one would say the *Kaddish yatom*, the "Mourner's *Kaddish*"; and the *halacha* lays out a strict hierarchy of priorities as to who that person would be.

The logic behind the rule requiring no more than one person to recite the *Kaddish*, is that—as a general Talmudic principle lays down—one cannot hear two people who are talking at the same time.

Faced by all the travails that the Jews had suffered, including the slaughter of all the Jews in an entire town or village, there were often cases where a multitude of people had an obligation to recite the *Kaddish*, and all felt the personal need to recite the prayer. This brought about a change in practice in many places, so that all mourners would recite *Kaddish* simultaneously. Here in the yeshiva, in well-ordered prayer services, the student told us, all the mourners recite the *Kaddish* in unison, as a chorus.

It was not that unusual. In some synagogues, as for example, the principal synagogue in the Israeli settlement of Alon Shvut, all those saying *Kaddish* stand behind the *bimah*—the altar from which the Torah is read—and recite together.

Our student friends then went on to tell us some interesting history involving Rabbi Kook and the *Kaddish*.[28] In 1924, bearing in mind the close ties between the People of Israel and the Land of Israel, Rabbi Kook, along with the ultra-Orthodox Rabbi Yosef Chaim Sonnenfeld, embarked on a mission to a number of non-religious kibbutzim. Although these kibbutzim were anything but observant of Jewish law, Rabbi Kook felt that the fact that they were engaged in building up and settling Eretz Israel was a great religious privilege, whether they accepted that fact or not.

When the rabbi was asked how he was able to deal with people who were so clearly non religious that they sometimes mocked the rules of Judaism, he replied: "In the *Kaddish*, we first ask for God's Name to be glorified (*yitgadal*), and only afterwards do we ask for it to be sanctified (*veyitkadash*).

"What this meant to Rabbi Kook is that first Eretz Israel must be glorified, by having it populated by Jews, and only afterwards do we need to work on sanctifying it, by converting these people into observant Jews."

In fact, the text of the opening of the *Kaddish* is from the prophet Ezekiel (38:23), "I will glorify Myself, and sanctify Myself, and I will make Myself known in the eyes of many nations; and they shall know that I am the Lord."

That verse referred to the falling of rain, a critical factor in making Eretz Israel bloom. Indeed we are told (Jerusalem Talmud, *Berachot* 9:3), that rain was so important an event in the lives of the farmers of Eretz Israel, that when it came they would say, "Magnified and sanctified and exalted be Your Name, our King, for each drop of rain which You cause to fall upon us."

Going deeper into the past, we remembered that the Shivat Tziyon movement, the forerunner of the Zionist movement, was believed by Rabbi Kook to be one that heralded the "beginning of the redemption" and that would herald the arrival of the Messiah.

"Does that mean that one may not reject any Jew?" we asked another yeshiva student. "Exactly," he replied. "In fact, the opposite is the case. One must do everything possible to bring everyone closer, and this applies especially to the *chalutzim* pioneers who are building up the land of Israel, even though they are far distant from religious observance. That was why Rabbi Kook became the leader of Religious Zionism. He was tolerant and worked at bringing those far away from Torah closer to it, but this was never at the expense of compromising his observance of even the most minor Jewish law or tradition."

Our visit to the Merkaz Harav Yeshivah came to an end. We had learned much more about the *Kaddish*. We also learned much more about the remarkable Rabbi Kook, his founding of the religious movement *Degel Yerushalayim* (the Flag of Jerusalem), his support of the Hebrew University, and his extensive writing and pervasive and continuing influence on the life and culture of Israel.[29]

We came away with great new insights into the *Kaddish*, which could best be summed up as: *Kaddish* offers us a recipe for life, teaching us that we may not delay our assigned tasks and the demands made upon us. It reminds us of an hourglass, where the sand inexorably runs down, where things which might appear to be minor are major and vice-versa; where one must admit one's mistakes, draw conclusions from them, and improve ones self accordingly, and where one must constantly evaluate life's priorities.

Kaddish and God's guardianship over us sends us a clear message: One should pursue life's goals and utilize one's potential to the utmost. One needs to be profoundly aware of the world in which we live, and one must not ignore that which one is able to accomplish.

Kaddish says to us, "Examine what options you have available to you, maintain an awareness of these, make proper choices, and bring about changes in your life while at the same time contributing to making the world a better place."

· 5 ·

SURVIVAL OF THE KADDISH NOTWITHSTANDING THE HOLOCAUST (SHO'AH)

*O*UR FINAL STOP in Jerusalem was brief, but meaningful. This was a visit to Yad Vashem, the official Holocaust memorial authority. This place stirs up emotion in every visitor.

There, we located a document in which, just before he was sent to the gas chambers, a father wrote to his son: "You are the only one of our family to stay alive, you are my *Kaddishl*" (a term sometimes used by Yiddish-speaking Jews about their children—i.e., the child who will say *Kaddish* after the parent's death).

What more could one say about the generation-to-generation flow of Jewish tradition? It was all there, in that one brief and tragedy-laden message.[30]

Orit, a guide in the "World of the Child" department of Yad Vashem, told us of another connection to *Kaddish*: In the Jewish world, the 27th day of the Hebrew month of *Nisan*, the 19th of April, the day of the uprising in the Warsaw Ghetto, is observed as "The Day of the Sho'ah and Heroism," or the "Holocaust Day," as it is referred to in English.

That day was established as an annual memorial day by the Israeli Knesset. The Chief Rabbinate of Israel, however, selected another day to commemorate the Holocaust, namely the fast day of the 10th of the Hebrew month of Tevet, which was made the "Universal *Kaddish* Day." On that day, in many synagogues, all the congregants together recite the *Kaddish yatom*—the "Mourner's *Kaddish*"—in memory of the six million Jews murdered by the Nazis and their accomplices.

The saying of the *Kaddish* after the Sho'ah is a collective acceptance of God's actions, especially given all the searing questions relating to faith or belief in God after the Sho'ah. It again stirs up the question of where was God while the six million were being murdered?

How could it happen? Six million Jews, many of them righteous, praying three times a day, were led into gas chambers. Those surviving had deep fundamental conflicts. Why did they survive while so many others of equal or greater worth perish?

If one accepts *Kaddish* as the ultimate prayer to God as the unquestioned "King of Kings" who can do no wrong, and decisions are made which cannot be questioned—then why pray at all? Of what value is prayer?

The answer offered by many rabbis is that one prays because the rules expressed in *Halacha* require it. Prayers are a must. They are a Jew's dues, his obligation. There is also some rabbinical thinking that prayer can be both on a personal level and a national level and that one should pray without expectations of personal reward.

In addition, there is the feeling that prayer is necessary to nourish the perennial hope that enough prayers in one's life will cause one's existence to become less jumbled and more blessed. In the author's opinion, this has become one of the fundamental issues of Judaic faith and has survived because of the *Kaddish*.

Rabbi Amram Gaon, in the 9th century C.E., wrote that when a mourner recites the *Kaddish*, he is thereby accepting God's decision as just. According to him, after a person is buried, the *chazan* recites the *Kaddish* as an acceptance of God's verdict. The same may apply to the saying of the *Kaddish* after the Sho'ah.

Indeed, even in the most horrendous times during this experience, Jews continued to keep alive a spark of Jewishness. Even while in the most trying of all the times in Jewish history, they still faithfully recited the *Kaddish*.

Although there remain, in rapidly diminishing number, survivors of the death camps, sixty years later, they may still be called the Sho'ah generation. The Sho'ah is very much with us, and has given added meaning and a new dimension to the *Kaddish*.

· 6 ·

A Study of Rabbi Levi Yitzchak of Berdishev as a Chassidic Force

*W*E DECIDED TO continue our quest about the *Kaddish* outside Israel. The history of the Jewish people is a fascinating one. What we had found about *Kaddish* up to this point already has woven a spellbinding mosaic. *Kaddish* is tied to much of Jewish history.

To learn about Kaddish throughout the world, we started in the Ukraine. This part of Eastern Europe produced some of Judaism's greatest rabbis and scholars. One of them, unique by any account, was Rabbi Levi Yitzchak of Berdichev who led Chassidism to become a major force among the Jews of central Poland, Lithuania, and the Ukraine. Our study of the life and death of Rabbi Yitzchak led to further new insights into the *Kaddish*.[31]

Rabbi Yitzchak was deeply involved in the daily life of the Jewish community, traveling throughout the country and teaching the masses of Jews to serve God with joy and zeal. He was renowned as a defender of the Jewish people and, on occasion, this defense was even invoked against God. His approach to religious practice was not always considered acceptable, and he often faced Jewish opponents who persecuted him.

His death was as unusual as his life; on Simkhat Torah in the Hebrew year of 5570 (1810) he danced with the Torah scroll the entire day, then collapsed and died with the scroll still sheltered in his arms. Rabbi Levi Yitzchak was renowned for his constant and steadfast defense of the Jewish people. He would take verses which were clearly critical of Jews and reinterpret them so as to make them sound like praise. He was able to discover a spiritual element in the most mundane of things and actions.

He declared that no matter how mundane the task a Jew was performing, deep down that Jew was really doing it to serve God. He expressed his attitude toward Jews as follows: "No person has the right to say anything bad about Jews. It is always our job to find the positive in every Jew." Further, "In theory, every Jew wants to serve God every single moment, even as the angels do. Unfortunately, the need to earn a living prevents him from doing so."

While persecution forced Rabbi Yitzchak to move from town to town, he finally found a home in Berdechev, a Ukranian city near Kiev. He remained there until his death, having served God for a long life, as they used to say, "in peace and love."

In the course of his studies, the rabbi composed a number

of musical compositions. These were melodies full of love for his fellow man, love of Jews and love of God. The songs he composed were unusual in that they were free-verse, not bound by any rhyme or meter. One example was the *"Kaddish"*[32] he wrote, as well as his famous *"Dudele"* (i.e., "You").

His *"Kaddish"* has many melodies in it: the melody of Talmud study, the weekday prayer melody, and the weekday *Kaddish*. This latter rendering is crystal-clear. When he prayed, Rabbi Levi Yitzchak saw himself as an attorney defending the entire Jewish People, and he would approach God on their behalf, often with tears and pleas, sometimes "speaking" to God as an equal, and sometimes even expressing complaints to God.

A collection of his lectures were printed in a volume entitled *Kedushat Levi*. These lectures were unusual in the simplicity of their approach. They are suffused with the sincere belief that whatever God does is for the good. Thus the *Kaddish* encourages Jews to believe that there is a Master of the Universe, and that in the long run everything is for the good.

If we look at his *"Kaddish,"* we discover a very unusual version, for Rabbi Levi Yitzchak is carrying on an argument with God! We find him talking to God as an equal. The text, translated from the blunt and almost shockingly colloquial Yiddish:

> *Good Morning, Lord of the Universe!*
> *I, Levi Yitzchak, son of Sarah, of Berdichev, have come to you*
> *To press charges against You, on behalf of Your people, Israel.*
> *What do You have against Your nation, Israel?*
> *And why have You started up with Your Nation, Israel?*
> *After all, on every matter (it states in the Torah), "Say to the*

Children of Israel."
On every matter: "Command the Children of Israel."
On every matter: "Speak to the Children of Israel."
Merciful Father in Heaven, how many nations are there in the
  world?
Persians, Babylonians, Edomites,
The Russians, what do they say?
"Our Czar is supreme."
The Germans, what do they say?
"Our kingdom is supreme."
The English, what do they say?
"Our empire is supreme."
But I, Levi Yitzchak, son of Sarah, say:
Yisgadal veyiskadash shemei rabbah.
And I will not move from my place
Until there is an end to all of this
And our exile will come to an end,
Yisgadal ve-yiskadash shemei rabbah.

The local Jews heard his words, sung with such great emotion, and they were all moved. Here was their rabbi speaking to God, and showing the nerve to argue with him! **Yisgadal ve-yiskadash shemei rabbah.**

This was the epitome of Rabbi Levi Yitzchak's ideas. We did not find either his home or his synagogue in Berdichev, but we did locate his grave; and as we stood around it, we understood how the simplicity of the *Kaddish* was so fitting for him.

We went from Berdichev, in the Ukraine, to Poland. In the town of Wiadislav, near Kielce, a group of young Chassidim of the sect of the Rebbe of Gur was totally isolated from their surroundings. They fortified themselves in a vacant attic and remained there day and night studying the Talmud, exactly as they had before the war. There were even private homes where great Torah scholars continued to give lectures on the Talmud to the starving, beaten Jews who flocked to them defying the Nazi edicts that forbade Torah study.

Another story: A distinguished family in the same town had a comfortable home and was forced to give up almost all of it, except for the kitchen. That single room was divided in two. Half was used by the family for its sleeping quarters. The other half was set aside for Torah study.

Gabriel Morgenstern, one of the few survivors of that family, described the scene. "In that small very cramped space, just a few square feet, young men and boys would gather several times a day. This was the schedule of my rebbe: at 4:30 a.m. he would teach the tractate *Yevamot*, with the commentaries of *Rashi* and *Tosafot*. From 6:30 p.m. to 10:00 p.m. he would teach the tractate *Shabbat*, with various commentaries, relating to the 39 forbidden categories of work on the Sabbath. In this room, one did not feel the heavy sense of doom that everyone felt. One might almost forget that there was a war right outside the doorstep."

Further research in Poland confirmed what we already knew, that the study of the Torah in Nazi-controlled Europe was not limited to the ghettos into which Jews had been forced. There was even Torah study in the concentration and extermination camps, with inevitable references to *Kaddish*.[33] In some camps, after a long day of back-breaking work and with starvation rations, there were Jews who conducted Torah classes in their barracks, lying on the wooden pallets that served as beds.

We have records of classes in Talmud, Mishnah, and the

Bible, being given in many of the concentration camps, with full knowledge that the penalty for teaching or studying Torah invariably was death! One scholar, Dr. Meir Dworzetski, describes Torah study in the camp where he had been sent: "In the horrendous camp of Dautmergen in southern Germany, a group of yeshiva students would assemble nightly to recite a chapter of the Mishnah before going to sleep on their vermin-infested pallets. They were exhausted, having spent the whole day laboring in the lime pits, along with the other prisoners.

They were on the verge of starvation not unlike their fellow prisoners. They were drenched to the skin from working in the trenches. They had not bathed for months and were infested with lice, just like the other prisoners. Yet an emaciated and pale young man from Novogorodsk would recite Mishnayot by heart, and the others would repeat each Mishnah after him.

After they finished studying, they would recite the *Kaddish d'rabbanan*, as is always done after ten men study together. When they recited the words, "Upon Israel and upon its rabbis…" in the *Kaddish d'rabbanan*, some eyes would be flooded with tears. Where were the people of Israel, and where were its rabbis? It is true that we all wanted to believe that everything that happens is the will of God and under His direct supervision, but how long would He allow the tyrants to continue their barbaric slaughter?

And in the academic journal *Sinai*, Dr. Dworzetski notes further: " Among the Torah activists in the Vilna Ghetto was a yeshiva student named Leibl Navorchik-Niaboshchik (possibly from the Ukraine): I was with him in camps in Estonia and in Germany, and I would join the Talmud classes which he would deliver orally to his friends in the camp. Once, as I was taken to the hospital suffering from blood poisoning, he comforted me and told me that I was not allowed to be afraid, and that if I did not come out alive from the hospital (in general, being admitted to the hospital was considered a death sentence) he promised that he would say *Kaddish* for me. By the time I was discharged from the hospital, he himself was no longer among the living."

Along with such *Kaddish* anecdotes, there were tales about those who had harsh questions for God. Often, these were defiant accusations against God: "Where were You, God?"

This was sometimes asked even by saintly men, who cried out at what had been done. Thus, the Rebbe of Fiartzenev, one of the great leaders of the Chassidic world, a gifted teacher and pedagogue, lived through the Holocaust, and when he came to say *Kaddish* he was simply unable to hold back his anguish. In July 1942, as he was being taken in a transport to Treblinka, from which he never returned, tears overcame him.

· 7 ·

CHASSIDIC CUSTOMS AND THOUGHTS IN MEMORIALIZING THE DECEASED

*A*N ANCIENT JEWISH custom exists which tells us to visit the graves of the saintly and to pray there for the welfare of the Jewish people and for one's individual welfare.[34] As *Rashi* notes on the verse (Genesis 48:7), "As for me, when I came from Padan, Rachel died in the land of Canaan in the road, when there was still some way to come to Efrat; and I buried her on the way to Efrat—namely Bethlehem."

Jacob told Joseph and Benjamin: "Even though I am bothering you to bring [my body] back for burial in the Land of Canaan, and I did not do so for your mother, for she died close to Bethlehem and I did not bring her into Bethlehem to bury her in Eretz Israel, and I know that you are upset with me [for not doing so], know that [what I did] was at [God's] command, so that [in the future] she will help her descendants. Thus, when Nevuzaradan exiled them and they passed that place, Rachel came out of her grave and cried and begged for mercy, as it states, (Jeremiah 31:15–16), 'A voice is heard in Ramah, lamentation, and bitter weeping, Rachel weeping for her children.'

And the Holy One, Blessed be He answers: 'Your work shall be rewarded, says the Lord; and they shall come back from the land of the enemy.'"

So to this day we go to Rachel's tomb and seek mercy for the Jewish people. So too, when the spies that were sent to Eretz Israel by Moses came to the land, we are told that "he came up to Hebron" (Numbers 13:22). Rashi wonders why the Torah states in the singular that *he* came up, and he answers, based on our sages, that "Caleb alone went there and prostrated himself at the tombs of our forefathers, praying that he would not be drawn after the other spies" (based on Sotah 34).

So tens of thousands of people go up to the grave of Rabbi Shimon Bar Yochai (the rabbi to whom the *Zohar*, the basic book of Kabbalah, is ascribed to) on the anniversary of his death, on *Lag Ba'Omer*. In Poland, too, tens of thousands of Jews would go to the graveside of Rabbi Moshe Isserles, the Rama,[35] as well as to the graves of other great rabbis in Poland.[36]

This is not in any way an attempt to call up the dead, but rather, as *Maharal* writes, the purpose is "to beg the Holy One, Blessed be He for mercy due to the merit of the saintly departed."

In the Holy Books, one finds many accounts of people going to the gravesides of the saintly. Thus, in Tractate *Ta'anit*

(16) it states specifically: "Why does one visit the cemeteries? So that the dead will appeal for mercy for us" when there is a need for rain. *Tosafot* states that that is the origin of the custom to visit the cemetery on *Tisha B'Av*, for *Tisha B'Av* is a communal fast, just as the fast which is held when the rain does not fall."

That same tractate (22) mentions Rabbi Mannes, son of Rabbi Jonah, who was persecuted by the officials of the entourage of the *Nasi* (the Exilarch—the head of the Jewish people after the Jews went into exile), and who prostrated himself on his father's grave and cried out, "Father! Father! These people are persecuting me."

And in Tractate *Bava Metzia* (85) we are told of a blind man who was cured of his blindness after having prayed at the cave of Rabbi Chiyya. So too do we find in Tractate *Berachot* (18) that rabbis who had financial woes had their problems solved after praying at the gravesides of great sages.

We also have accounts of a sage who lost his memory and who went to the graveside of Rabbi Shimon Bar Yochai to beg him to teach him Torah. It is this need of people to go to the graves of our sages that resulted in many of such gravesites having a small building built on them, to enable people to enter and pray, especially on the anniversary of the sage's death.

Chassidic circles state that the grave of a famous sage has the same sanctity as that of Eretz Israel. Rabbi Nachman of Bratslav went so far as to say that just as certain sins can be rectified by one's being in Eretz Israel, the same applies to those who go to the graves of great sages.

A Chassidic tale relates that Rabbi Nachum of Chernobyl went to the graveside of the Ba'al Shem Tov[37] on a very cold winter day, with only socks on his feet. He said that he did not feel any cold at all because the Ba'al Shem Tov's grave is like Eretz Israel, and it is not cold there. (*Sefer HaBesht* I, pp. 16, 79).

Rabbi Aharon of Karlin[38] expressed his distress at the fact that people did not come to the grave of his grandfather, Rabbi Aharon the Great, whereas many people came to pray and plead at the graves of the great rabbis in Wohlin, a district of Poland. It is known that the Rebbe of Lubavich, would visit the grave of his father-in-law, the previous Rebbe, and would read all the *kvitlach* (letters sent to him for his advice and aid). Indeed, if anyone asked the Rebbe to pray for him, he would reply, "I will do so at the graveside." He, too, would visit his father-in-law's grave wearing only socks, even in the winter.

In addition to the custom of visiting graves on *Tisha B'Av*. It is also customary to do so during the month of *Elul* and on the day before Rosh Hashanah. Another Chassidic tale notes that Rabbi Mordechai of Chernobyl visited the graves of Rabbi Zusya of Hanipol and Rabbi Leib of Hanipol, near the grave of the Maggid of Mezrich, and said that the smell there was the sweet smell of the Garden of Eden.

Regarding the righteous that have died, King Solomon said, "I laud the righteous who have already died," because now that they are dead they are in the Garden of Eden (*Ta'amei Ha'Minhagim*).

Then there was the *Kaddish* of the Rebbe of Karlin, who was killed in the Sho'ah. At the end of the Hebrew month of *Iyyar*, 5699 (May, 1939), Rabbi Avraham Elimelech, the Rebbe of Karlin, visited Eretz Israel for the fourth time. We may note that on his second trip to the country, he lost all of his personal documents, including his passport, and it was only through the intervention of Rabbi Kook that he was able to disembark even though he did not have a single identifying document. The rabbi was renowned for his nobility of character, and the contentment which radiated from him, and especially for the close ties between him and each of his followers. When the ship approached the dock, many of his Chassidim were waiting to greet him, just as in former times the residents of Jerusalem would wait to welcome people bringing their first fruits to the Temple.

Every car sent to greet him had been polished, and all awaited the Rebbe expectantly. As soon as he set foot on the gangplank, the Chassidim broke out in a joyous song and dance, inviting the dock workers to join them.

Despite all the excitement, the Rebbe did not join in. His face was solemn, even grave, as he descended the gangplank. As soon as he landed, he ordered everyone to stop singing. Then he asked them in Yiddish, "How can you sing when Poland is burning?"

When the Rebbe realized that his Chassidim did not know what he meant—for they thought everything in Poland was peaceful and quiet—he told them, in a voice filled with emotion: 'I have come here to pray and to plead at the graves of the righteous because of the situation of the Jews in Poland."

The Chassidim were convinced that, as on the previous occasions, the Rebbe would travel to Jerusalem, but he immediately disabused them of that idea: "I am traveling to the Galilee right now," he said, "to pray at the graves of the righteous there." He asked his followers not to speak about the impending catastrophe in Poland.

Some of them were convinced that the Rebbe was temporarily deranged, possibly because of his long and arduous voyage. Every time he tried to address them, he broke into a prolonged and bitter bout of weeping.

When the party arrived in Meron, where Rabbi Shimon Bar Yochai is buried, Rabbi Avraham Elimelech asked to be left in solitude at the grave. Then he instructed his attendants to close the door to the grave building, so that no one would be able to enter while he was there.

The Chassidim, curious, tried to hear what the Rebbe was saying, but all they heard was sobbing and weeping.

A similar thing happened that night, when he visited the grave of the Ari[39] in Safed. As the Chassidim waited for the Rebbi to finish reciting the Psalms, he burst out of the structure and said, "We have not accomplished a thing! We have not accomplished a thing! Say *Kaddish*, and stress the greatness of God in His world."

By now, the Eretz Israel Chassidim were unable to restrain themselves, and a delegation came to him and said: "Rebbe, how can you say such things? On what do you base your terrible prophecies?"

The Rebbe looked them straight in the eye and said: "I have in my possession a letter from the Ba'al Shem Tov in which he gives a detailed account of what will happen, up to the time of the Messiah."

"I would like to see that letter," said one of the Chassidim.

The Rebbe told him, "If you see it, you will be driven insane."

Indeed throughout the time the Rebbe remained in Eretz Israel, a period of more than two months, he kept talking about the great calamity awaiting Polish Jewry. The Chassidim kept hoping that the Rebbi's mood would finally change and that he would brighten up.

Meanwhile, he kept repeating: "Say *Kaddish*, and stress the greatness of God in His world."

A few days before he returned to his home at Karlin, and while he was still surrounded by his followers in Jerusalem, the Rebbe began giving his most personal possessions to the elders among them. They in turn regarded this as a terrible sign of an eternal parting and they begged and pleaded with him not to go back.

"Stay in Eretz Israel," they cried.

The Rebbe, though, who had come alone, refused to abandon his family in Karlin, and insisted on returning.

Thus, it was at the dockside in Haifa that the Chassidim had to part from their beloved Rebbe. As they waited while he embarked, the ship's whistle sounded, signaling that the ship was about to leave. The Rebbe's assistant told them, "We are late; we must leave now."

The Rebbe, tears streaming down his face, said to his audience in a broken voice, "I wish I had not been so late, but say *Kaddish* and stress the greatness of God in His world." He then walked up the gangplank to the ship.

When the Sho'ah began, a number of the Rebbe of Karlin's followers sought to save him and his family using a route that would take them through Vilna, which was known to be secure. For weeks the Rebbe refused to consider it, but in the end was persuaded.

Arrangements were made at the very last minute to have him and his family escape. When the Rebbe and his family were already in the car, one man ran to him and asked him,

"For whom have you left us?" When the Rebbe heard this, he got out and returned home. He ascended to heaven along with his whole community. May God avenge his death.[40]

In the cellars of the Rebbe's home in Karlin there were very valuable collections which he had inherited from his forebears, including the copy of the *Zohar* which had belonged to the Ba'al Shem Tov, a few hairs of his beard, as well as various ancient manuscripts, religious objects, and silver items, all of which had belonged to disciples of the Ba'al Shem Tov. Not one of these items remains, except for a single old *Siddur* which had a bookmark in place at the *Kaddish*.

On one side of the Warsaw Jewish cemetery there is a very elaborate tombstone indicating the last resting place of the very wealthy Rabbi Berke, who was known for his philanthropy. The tombstone is made of the finest marble, and the decorations are a true work of art. On the tombstone one finds engraved the verse, "By the rivers of Babylon" and underneath it a picture of a river, a bridge, and towers.

Berke was the son of Rabbi Yosef Shmuel. He was born in the Praga district of Warsaw. Some references to him call him "Shmuelewitz" (i.e., the son of Shmuel), while in *The City-Dwellers and the Jews in Poland,* he is referred to as Berke Yoselditz (Berl, son of Yosl). The book discusses at length the battalion of 500 Jewish cavalry that Berke established in Warsaw.

Rabbi Shmuel, was known throughout Poland as a wealthy man who gave a great deal to charity. It is said that when the Cossacks defeated the Polish army, Rabbi Shmuel asked the Russian minister of war to issue a proclamation among his soldiers, that every soldier who would bring Rabbi Shmuel a live Jew would be paid a ruble, and a smaller amount would be paid for each dead Jew. That proclamation was indeed made, and as a result Rabbi Shmuel managed to gather around him a large number of Jews who would otherwise have been murdered, while Jews who had been killed and who might not otherwise have had a Jewish funeral, were now given one.

Rabbi Shmuel kept his word, and spent almost all his fortune in order to redeem his pledge.

There is another tale about Rabbi Shmuel. The Rebbe of Gur, the *Chiddushei HaRim*,[41] once related that whenever the Maggid of Koznitz was the *chazan* on the Sabbath, when he reached the *Kaddish* all his followers would burst into song, while he would just say the words. In the year 5564 (1804), though, when they reached the *Kaddish*, the Maggid began a different melody, a very beautiful one. Nobody else knew the *niggun*,[42] so they were unable to sing along.

After the prayers, the Maggid noticed the confusion of the Chassidim, and he explained to them: "It is about three years since Rabbi Shmuel of Praga died. After his death, a number of the prosecuting angels spoke out against him for various sins he had committed, but what he had done in saving Jews and causing other Jews to have a Jewish burial outweighed all his sins, and it was decreed that he should go to the Garden of Eden. However, he still had to atone for his sins, which took three years. At this very time he is on the way to the Garden of Eden, and the exquisite melody just heard is what the angels sang as they escorted him there."

There is a mystical interpretation that the *Kaddish* recited on Saturday evening is thought to help your relatives to remain in the Garden of Eden.

· 8 ·

ANCILLARY EFFECTS OF THE KADDISH

$\mathcal{F}$ROM POLAND WE moved to Prague, the capital of the Czech Republic. It is one of the most beautiful cities in the world.

We set out for the Jewish Quarter, one of the magnets that draw millions of tourists to the city each year. In the middle of the Quarter is a cemetery which is one of the most interesting in all of Europe. Because of the great shortage of land from which the Jewish community always suffered, twelve layers of graves are placed, one atop another.

In the middle of this cemetery is the grave of the Maharal, Rabbi Judah Loew B. Betzalel, one of the great rabbis of the

16th century (1525–1609). The aforementioned Rabbi Kook was in many ways the spiritual heir of the *Maharal*, even though he lived centuries later. He was heir for the love of Israel and the yearning for redemption and mysticism. The *Maharal* also had a profound influence on the Chassidic Movement as well as on the famous "*gaon* (genius) of Vilna."

We walked through this area as if mesmerized, for there is no other place to compare with it in the Jewish world. We went into the Altneushul. To get to this synagogue, which dates back hundreds of years, one must descend a few steps, in accordance with the verse, "Out of the depths I called You."

As we walked down the steps, before entering the synagogue proper, we heard two explanations for its name. One is that the words simply mean the "old-new synagogue." Another explanation was given by an Israeli scholar who happened to be present during our visit. According to her, the word *altneushul* (which in German means Old Synagogue) is transliterated into Hebrew and gets a different meaning—i.e. the synagogue is the "al-Tnay" synagogue, a "conditional" synagogue. This interpretation is based on a legend about a bare rock in the building. According to the story, this rock was originally part of the Temple in Jerusalem. It was placed there "conditionally," in that once the Temple is rebuilt the rock will be returned.

There is another explanation for the words "Al Tnay" which actually is related to the golem legend. One Shabbat, the *Maharal* forgot to take out God's name from the golem's mouth, and fearing that he would create havoc, the *Maharal* voided the Kabbalat Shabbat since it was brought in "Al Tnay."

The *Maharal* of Prague exemplifies a sincere strain of hope and pure faith in the Jewish tradition. When the Jews were attacked repeatedly, he is reputed, in the famous legend, to have created a golem; a creature formed out of clay, and an amulet imprinted with God's ineffable name was put into the golem's mouth causing it to come to life.

The legend further tells us that the golem served both the *Maharal*[43] and the Jewish people. The golem was mainly used to defend the beleaguered Jews of Prague (as an example of the treatment of the Jews, one can find the statue of Jesus crucified on the Charles Bridge over the Vltava River, on which are carved the words, "Holy, holy, holy" by a Jew who was forced to do so after he had been accused of spitting at the statue. Similarly, there is a gilded image of Jesus' passion in the Church of Our Lady before Tyn, which vividly depicts the ascendancy of the Christians and the subjugation of the Jews.

The present rabbi of the Altneushul is a convert, Rabbi Sidon. He studied for the rabbinate in Jerusalem, was ordained, and then returned to Prague, where today there are about 5,000 Jews. We spoke to him about the *Kaddish* and our quest.

Before addressing the principal subject, Rabbi Sidon gave us some history on his role as the leader and rabbi of the *Maharal*'s synagogue, though he began by talking about a curiosity. Across from the synagogue, on the wall of the community building, is a large clock with Hebrew letters rather than numerals on its face. Even more remarkable, the clock hands run in a counter-clockwise direction.

We remembered an old legend, "Every hour on the face of a clock is like ten years of a person's life." Thus, the entire course of man's life is 120 years. Up to the age of 60, one's life passes slowly as the hour hand of the clock moves downward. From age 60 on, the hands of the clock start moving upward, at what seems to be a much faster rate. So it is with one's life, when time seems to speed by as one ages.

After the age of 60, one's infirmities become progressively worse. The question arises: "How should one act once one has passed the age of 60? What one needs to do is to constantly reset the clock to the correct time."

Rabbi Sidon laughed and said, "Here, the clock runs backward!"

Under the same community building, the Rabbi told us, was a large cellar packed with thousands of Jewish religious objects. This is a vast treasure trove for the Jewish people, possibly one of the greatest collections of its kind in the Jewish world. The collection has been warehoused there ever since the end of World War II.

The Germans were convinced that they could taste victory and that by war's end they would have wiped out all the Jews in all the countries under their control. This was according to the plans drawn at the infamous Wannsee Conference, in 1942.

They wanted to document that Jews were an "inferior race" which they would destroy and then memorialize in a "museum of the vanished Jewish race." They sent truckloads of plundered Jewish objects which they seized in territories under their control. These included Torah scrolls, Menorahs, *siddurim*, Hebrew holy books, spice boxes for *havdalah*, exquisite *kiddush* cups, ritual circumcision kits, *tefillin*, *tallitot*, etc.

The various items were sorted and classified with typical German "efficiency." After the war, all these items became the property of the Czech government.[44]

After this discussion, we came to talk of the *Kaddish*. On Holocaust Memorial Day, Rabbi Sidon recites the *Kaddish*, not in the synagogue, but in the communal building, which has listed on its walls thousands of names of Jews killed by the Nazis. Many of the Jews were killed in Terezinstat, the concentration camp only an hour outside of Prague. Another memorial in the building is an exhibit of drawings by Jewish children who were later murdered by the Germans; drawings of butterflies and of nature, one of them with the touching caption: "I never saw a butterfly again."

Rabbi Sidon also told us about a special *Kaddish* which he introduced and which has an added reference to Jerusalem. (Prague has often been called the Jerusalem of Europe.) The new words were added to the *Kaddish* in recognition of the aforementioned legend of the rock that was brought from the Temple in Jerusalem.

Our conversation led to a much longer consideration of Jewish history before returning to our interest in the *Kaddish*. We talked about the times after the destruction of the Second Temple, when the entire tenor of Jewish life changed. Life became sadder. Indeed, after the Temple was destroyed, all the additional fast days—as well as additional feast days—came to an end.

Even the Torah-mandated festivals lost much of their luster after the Temple was destroyed, and with it the opportunity to celebrate each festival in the Temple itself. Most Jews were forced to live outside the Land of Israel, the very source of much joy in life and of many of Judaism's ancient customs.

The Jews were fortunate in that after the Temple was destroyed the sages of Kerem D'Yavneh[45] became leaders as the people reformulated much of Jewish law and custom. They based what they did on principles which were applicable to the new circumstances. These included practices meant to keep the memory of the Temple and Jerusalem alive, along with prayers for the restoration of the Temple. These practices were designed to dispel the deep gloom into which all had sunk and to enable them to look more hopefully to the future. It provided for the continuity of the Jewish religion. All these customs have been enshrined in both the Jerusalem and Babylonian Talmud as well as the later works of the great rabbis of the post-Talmudic period.

New prayers were added, expressing a hunger for redemption and for a return to Zion, for the rebuilding of the Temple, and for the coming of the Messiah. The rabbis also decreed that when praying, one must face Jerusalem. Additions were made to the prayers of Biblical verses or verse fragments, which expressed a longing for Jerusalem and for the return from exile.[46]

In another display of longing for the restoration of the Temple and the fact that no celebration can be complete until such time, it is often customary for a groom at his wedding to put a little ash on his forehead, signifying mourning for the Temple.

In the *sheva berachot* ("seven blessings") at a wedding end, we find the words: "Let the childless one rejoice and revel when her children are gathered into her midst, blessed are You, O Lord, who makes the groom and bride joyful." And in the last blessing, we read, "Speedily, O Lord our God, may there be heard in the cities of Judah and in the courtyards of Jerusalem the sound of rejoicing and gladness."

And finally some added the following words to the *Kaddish*: "Rebuild the city of Jerusalem and raise up the Temple in it." The Altneushul, in our day, adopted this text, awaiting the rock being returned to Jerusalem. It is understood that, when the Temple is finally standing, the added words will be removed.

In Prague, we heard a story set in Jerusalem which gives additional substance to what we have called the "mystery" of the *Kaddish*.[47] In fact, this tale has elements of a true mystery—and romance as well.

Some years ago, we were told, the Jews of Jerusalem, even the most assimilated Jews in the city, much less the religious, were astonished when Milcah, the wife of one Rabbi Lamdan and mother of their two sons, fell in love with Ahmed Nasib, a merchant who was a member of one of the city of Hebron's most prominent Arab families. Ahmed Nasib had seen her in a shop one day and then and there fell in love and decided to woo her. She in turn was attracted and fell in love as well. Milcah, who hailed from a long and distinguished line of rabbis, finally decided that she could not live torn between two worlds, and resolved that she would follow Ahmed Nasib to Hebron.

When she told her husband of her decision, he was stunned.

"And the children? What will become of the children?" he pleaded. "What will we tell them: that their mother left them to live in Hebron as a Muslim?"

But his words were to no avail. "Tell the children I will always love them," were her parting words. Within a month a *get* (the Jewish divorce decree) was granted.

Soon thereafter, Milcah converted to Islam and was married to Ahmed.

Rabbi Lamdan prayed at the Western Wall, and fully expected much suffering for his ex-wife. But nothing of the kind happened. On the contrary, Milcah bore a number of sons and daughters to Ahmed Nasib, and was welcomed by all her neighbors as a devout Muslim. Rabbi Lamdan was forced to raise his two sons on his own, and they were told that their mother died when they were young.

For all practical purposes, Milcah was a devout Muslim—with one exception. She begged her Muslim husband to arrange for her sons, the sons of Rabbi Lamdan, to recite *Kaddish* for her after her death. "That way, I have not completely turned my back on the religion into which I was born," she said. She even went so far as to check with Jewish authorities in Hebron about how to be positive this would happen.

"Light Sabbath candles every Friday before sunset," she was told. "That will ensure that your sons will say *Kaddish* for you."

Milcah did not have any candles, but olive oil was abundantly available, so each Friday afternoon, before sunset, she would set up two lights in her window.

Ahmed Nasib and their children saw what she did, but did not object. They realized that Milcah needed at least one way to display her Jewishness. So it went on, year after year. Milcah's children grew up and left her home. Then, she was struck by tragedy. Ahmed died. Suddenly, all her Muslim "friends" turned away from her. They had never forgotten, it seemed, that Ahmed had married "the Jewish woman."

Of course, by this time Milcah's sons in West Jerusalem, Yakir and Shimon, had also grown up and turned out to be very capable businessmen, trading many varieties of goods in many different places. At one point, they became involved in a major business deal with an Arab in Hebron. The deal promised an enormous profit for both sides.

The brothers traveled to Hebron to cement the deal, but it

was a Friday, and as they negotiated, they did not notice the passage of time. There was no way they could get back to Jerusalem for the Sabbath, so they looked for a Jewish home to take them in.

They walked rapidly toward the Jewish quarter, but before they reached it they saw two lights burning in a window. Rather fearfully, they knocked on the door. They were greeted very warmly by the lady of the house, and even behind her veil they could see the broad smile on her face.

"Come in, come in!" the woman, who looked typically Arab, said.

They spent Sabbath in the home, and were treated royally. The woman even arranged for them to eat all three meals with a religious Jewish family living nearby. Of course the strange Muslim woman was their mother, Milcah. She had immediately recognized the brothers as her sons, but did not divulge her secret to them.

After the Sabbath, Milcah decided she would reveal her true identity. But, amazingly, tragedy struck like a lightning bolt. She suddenly clutched at her throat and died within minutes. All attempts to revive her were to no avail.

The neighborhood women, hearing the commotion, came in. When they saw she was dead, they told Yakir and Shimon, "She's a filthy Jew. We won't bury her. You take her with you and bury her. She always wanted to be buried among the Jews," they said.

Yakir and Shimon considered. "She still had a spark of Jewishness in her," said one. "After all, she did light the Sabbath candles, which led us to her."

So they saw to it that the body was carried away, still not knowing that this was their mother. They buried her on the

Mount of Olives, just beyond the Jewish cemetery. The brothers felt that what they had done was to somehow purify this strange woman who had lived as a Muslim all those years. After the burial, they decided it was only fitting to say *Kaddish*, so they gathered together a *minyan* of men and both said *Kaddish*[48] by the graveside.

That night, the brothers went back to their father and told him what had happened in Hebron and in Jerusalem. Rabbi Lamdan listened attentively, and when they had finished he burst into tears: "That was your mother," he sobbed. He then told them the full story of his first wife.

At first, the brothers were frozen in silence. Finally, they began to talk. They marveled at how they had been instrumental in assuring their mother's burial as a Jew. And, in the end, they said *Kaddish* for her for the next eleven months.

This extraordinary story, though true, has assumed proportions of myth, both among the Jews of Jerusalem and Hebron. It is the strange story of a family, torn apart by one kind of emotion, brought together by another, and finally brought to peace by the *Kaddish* tradition.

· 9 ·

Kaddish and Women

OUR RESEARCH INTO the *Kaddish* in the Diaspora led us to a book by Rabbanit Pninah Miller, *Harav Sheli* (My Rabbi).[49] In its pages, we see for the first time the importance of gender and the *Kaddish*.

The key to this is in Miller's re-telling of a story that she calls "The *Kaddish* of a Woman." This is how it begins:

> For two years the School of Hillel debated a basic issue: 'Is it better that Man was created, or would it have been better if Man had not been created?' In the end they decided that it would have been better had Man not been created.

"In other words, even in the case of the son of a wealthy man who lives in a palace, it would have been better had he not been created. This is all the more true in the case of a poor orphan girl who was born in a forsaken village in the Carpathian Mountains in Rumania.

As soon as I opened my eyes and began to think for myself, I realized that I had started life on the wrong foot," she said. "In those days, like all children, I was on good terms with God, and a number of times I asked Him: 'Why wasn't I born in the home of a British lord? And why was I born a girl rather than a boy? And why was I born to a father who is a Chassid?'

Rabbanit Miller continues: "In those days, in homes where the father wore a *shtreimel* (a hat worn on Sabbath and holidays by Chassidim), each son who was born was seen as the potential Messiah, through whom salvation would come for the family, and indeed for the entire Jewish people. That was why a male child was spoiled the same way the heir to a throne is spoiled.

"However, if a girl was born (God forbid!) she was treated with scorn and regarded as a monster who could only cause trouble, and who would be incorrigible from the very start. From the moment of birth there was a major difference, the difference between light and darkness, between *Purim* and *Tisha B'Av*, between a male and a female infant. The birth of a daughter brought unhappy notoriety to a family, while the birth of a son raised the family's stature in the community.

"On the Friday night before a boy's circumcision, neighbors, friends, and those who prayed in the same synagogue or in the same village, gathered together at the home of the mother for the *shalom zachar*,[50] to welcome the new soul sent down from Heaven.

"The guests would eat *arbes* (boiled chickpeas) and other delicacies, and would sing Sabbath songs, until the child's mother felt faint. They would put up a rope around the mother's bed and attach sheets to it, to "shield" the mother from the Evil Eye.

"For eight days the house was like a beehive; a dozen or so old and saintly volunteer women from the neighborhood would bring an assortment of amulets and charms to ward off the Evil Eye, while other women would come only to visit.

"Before the *shalom zachar*, the women would prepare enough honey cake and other sweets to cover the table. The evening before the circumcision, groups of little boys would come from all the Talmud Torah schools in the area, and would sing the *Shema* in unison at the newborn's crib. After them would come men of the neighborhood, to remain with the child until midnight and thereby ward off the Evil Eye.[51]

"As further safeguards, the men would hang prayer excerpts at every window, and place a Torah scroll binder underneath the newborn's pillow. The day of the circumcision was like a festival for all the synagogues in the village, for the prophet Elijah was said to attend each circumcision. The ceremony would reach its climax at the main synagogue where all the village notables would gather, to attend the induction of another member of the tribe into the Covenant of Our Father Abraham, peace be upon him.

"At that time, a group of pious women would bring in the infant, covered with a silk blanket over his diaper. The atmosphere was festive: each congregant carried a burning candle. The head of the Chassidic center was honored as the *sandak* ("godfather") while the local rabbi and the rabbinic court judge were both assigned tasks as part of the circumcision ritual. After the ceremony, a festive meal would be held, at which liquor flowed freely.

"By contrast, what happened when (God forbid!) a daughter was born? Nothing. No visitors. No refreshments. No Sabbath songs and no old folks with charms, no children reciting the *Shema*. Not even a bed sheet partition around the mother, because a woman who had given birth to a "monster" had no right to be protected from the Evil Eye. And there was no need to welcome the arrival of this new soul.

"It was not a time for celebration.

"If the relatives and neighbors met the new father in the marketplace or at the synagogue, they would not shake his hand, but would say *mazal tov* to him weakly and in an undertone, as if it were *Tisha B'Av*. And his enemies would say *mazal tov* very coldly and with malignant smiles.

"Nor would that be the end of the humiliation. On the Sabbath, when the father of the newborn daughter was called up to the Torah to give his new daughter a name, the congregants would bang on the benches and prayer stands, as one does on *Purim* when the evil Haman's name is mentioned."

Rabbanit Miller continued, recounting her personal experience: "When I was born, children were not handled in the sterile and cruel way they are today. Now the infant is taken into his or her new room, placed in a crib, the lights are turned off, the parents say, 'Good night,' and the child is left alone in the dark.

"Imagine the inhumanity in treating a newborn in such a

cruel and unfeeling way at a time when the infant is sensitive and fearful of everything around her. .

"Years before, a new mother would rock the baby to sleep, while singing traditional Jewish lullabies. Those were among the most precious moments in the infant's life. Thus, when I was born, I enjoyed plentiful mother's milk, and enchanting, sweet songs.

"After I was toilet-trained, my father took me to the study hall of the Chassidim. For me, it was a festival, because I was introduced there to new songs and melodies. As a little girl, I was enchanted with melodies the worshippers would sing, like "*Lecha dodi*" and the way they would dance each Friday evening while welcoming the Sabbath service.

"Looking back, I remember being especially impressed by the *se'udah shelishit*, the "third meal" of the Sabbath, where Jews with long beards and *shtreimels* or black hats would sing Sabbath songs as the sun disappeared from the horizon and night began to blanket us.

"They would sit at tables covered with liquor and herring, they would repeat Torah passages and tell stories of the great and saintly Chassidic rabbis, through whose merits, they believed, the world survives.

"When the Sabbath ended, they recited *havdalah*. When the *havdalah* text notes that 'the Jews had light and rejoicing,' the lights in the synagogue would all be lit, and the sudden burst of light would blind the eyes of the worshipers.

"I enjoyed the *se'udah shelishit* not only because of the moving Chassidic melodies, but also because of the small wheat *challot* which were baked just for the Sabbath. Let me explain. You see, the Marmaros area, where we lived, was poor and mountainous. We lived in constant poverty, and the whole week long we ate corn flour bread. At the *se'udah shelishit*, when I sat on my father's lap in the dark, I was able to reach out with my little hands and eat my fill of the wheat *challot*.

"About 2,000 years ago, the Sages of the Talmud stated that 'the world cannot survive without males and cannot survive without females, and yet happy is the person who has sons and woe to the person who has daughters.'

"As long as I can remember, I loved my father dearly, but I always felt that in his eyes, I was a constant reminder of the 'woe' of the Talmud. When my brother acted roughly and hit me and I went to my father to make peace between us, he never ruled according to what was right. He always acted unfairly, because he loved my brother so much. "I had no recourse, I accepted things as they were and I kept quiet about the blatant discrimination in our home, which was confirmed a hundred times each day, in words and action.

"One thing bothered me, and I was inconsolable about it, and that was at our Sabbath meals my brother would always receive the chicken leg from my father, while all I was given was the wing. . . . I was also hurt by the fact that my brother, the '*Kaddishl*,'[52] would receive a coin whenever he was examined by my father on the Talmud and performed well.

"My brother used the coin to buy chocolates. He would give me only a small bite. I cried and cried. I wanted to study Torah myself, to earn money, and to buy chocolates. In the end, my father gave in and allowed me to learn certain pages of the *siddur* by heart, including those such as the Grace after Meals.

"My victory was short-lived, because one day my father said: 'Enough! That's it! A daughter has no more to learn! Indeed, our sages say that 'One who teaches his daughter Torah teaches her licentiousness.'

"I burst into tears and asked, 'What then is man's enjoyment and his purpose in life if not to study and to acquire knowledge?' 'You have much to learn,' said my father consolingly. 'You must learn from your mother how to run a home, how to cook, to bake, to make the beds, to wash the floor, to clean the dishes, to weave, to knit.'

"I was in a state of despair. I was confronting the great dilemma of my life. What was I to do? Should I accept my father's verdict and return to the kitchen, or should I engage in a forlorn battle with him? And what is more painful than going into battle against the person you love most in the world?

"This was quite distressing for a girl of eleven. At night, my pillow was soaked with tears. One night I thought of my grandfather in Spinka, who loved me dearly, and who would tell me stories. Once, he told me a *midrash* the meaning of which was that for everything negative God created in the world, He created something positive, in order to comfort people. For example, the dark of the night can be terrifying, but the moon and stars brighten up the darkness; thorns hurt, but roses delight; lions and snakes scare us, but birds and butterflies are calming; strangers are apathetic about a little girl, but her parents are ready to give their lives for her.

"My father emigrated to Israel, served as a rabbi and taught Torah, but he died when he was still young. When I emigrated to Israel, a decade later, we—my brother and I—went to his graveside in Zichron Meir. My brother hung back, as he is a *cohen*, and said some of the Psalms and the *Kaddish*.

"I walked right up to the grave and 'spoke' to my father. This is what I said to him: 'The elders of Spinka did not come to greet my soul when I was born, nor did the little children sing the *Shema* at my crib. During my childhood, I was given only the chicken wing, and I was educated in a modern high school. In spite of that, my dear father, I fulfilled your dreams, married according to Jewish tradition and in the spirit of the Torah. With the help of a matchmaker I married a bearded yeshiva student, with a long, black *kapota* (a traditional Chassidic coat)."

Rabbanit Miller closes, writing: "That was my *Kaddish*," 5721 (1961).[51]

This story is a reflection of a prior age in Judaism. In Conservative and Reformed Judaism women lead prayers. They say *Kaddish,* and are called to the Torah in what is referred to as an egalitarian minyan. Even modern Orthodox synagogues will find women voluntarily saying *Kaddish* although not counting in the minyan, seated separately behind a *mechitza* (barrier).[53] This is a fairly new happening and reflects a change in the woman's role in Orthodox Judaism which is halachicly approved but was culturally repressed. Self-empowerment of Orthodox women has transformed many of the rituals which were undertaken only by men and has become part and parcel of that sect of Judaism. The inroads have been huge and probably would be unheard of until the last 25 years. It is an evolving process always within *Halacha* which is allowing women to participate in many formally restricted areas of the practice of their Judaism.

· 10 ·

CHASSIDISM, KADDISH, AND KOTZK

*O*UR NEXT DESTINATION was Kotzk,[55] a tiny village near Lublin, the home of the "Seer of Lublin" and of the famous Yeshivat Chachmei Lublin, founded by Rabbi Meir Shapiro. It was Rabbi Shapiro who originated the *Daf Yomi* concept, whereby Jews throughout the world study the same Talmudic page each day. If one flies from New York to Alaska, with stops along the way, one would find study groups of the *Daf Yomi* all on the same page, day by day.

While Lublin is home to many great rabbis, Kotzk is known for only one, but that rabbi created a new and unique genre of Chassidism, and his brilliant sayings enrich us to this day. Rabbi Menachem Mendl of Kotzk, next to whose hut we stood, was a man whose brilliant intellect was coupled with the purest of souls.

Here it was that he coined such provocative sayings as, "There is nothing as whole as a broken heart," and "There is nothing as crooked as a straight ladder." He was constantly searching for the truth; telling his disciples that they should reveal their sins publicly, while hiding their performance of the commandments.

In Kotzk, Rabbi Mendl spurned visitors who came from throughout Poland to study with him. He said: "Give me 150 worthy men and I will go with them from place to place and we will proclaim, 'This is my God and I will glorify Him.'"

In Kotzk, Jews prayed when their souls moved them rather than at the prescribed times. The Rabbi of Kotzk loathed materialism and money. (It is said that the first time he received a donation of money for his yeshiva, he said, "Feh!" From then on, he was unable to look at money except with loathing.)

About 200 years before the French existentialist Jean Paul Sartre, the Kotzker Rabbi, in his little village far away from the mainstream, said, 'If I am I because I am I, and you are you because you are you, then I am I and you are you. However, if I am I because you are you and you are you because I am I, then I am not I and you are not you."

When more and more Chassidim came to him, he drove them off, saying, "Do you think I am a chimney sweep? The whole week you are involved in theft, trickery, and dishonest dealings, and then you come to me on the Sabbath to be pardoned for your sins?"

A major rift in Chassidism developed as a result of this.

The Kotzker Rabbi rebuffed all those who came to him for material help. Rabbi Yosef Leiner, one of his disciples, did not agree with this extreme stand. He said, "Rebbe, these people come to you after a hard day working in the fields to receive a little blessing from you, some Torah learning, a little liquor and joy, and you turn them away because they are not Torah scholars? Let them join you and receive a little pleasure. They traveled long and far to be with you."

The legend is that Rabbi Leiner said this to Rabbi Mendl on a Friday night. The Kotzker Rabbi became angry and waved his hands so violently that he extinguished the Sabbath lights. Afterwards he went into his room, and did not emerge until his death. From time to time he opened the door to make a statement, which was transcribed by his disciples. He would then immediately shut the door. One of his most famous sayings, still resonant today, is: "There is no such thing as following the middle path. Only horses walk in the middle of the road. People walk at the side."

Brest-Litovsk, known as Brisk to the Jews of the region, was famous as the site of the signing of the treaty that ended World War I on the Eastern Front. For the Jews, the city was famous as a center of intellectual and cultural activity. For modern Israelis, Brisk is important as the birthplace of Menachem Begin who, along with David Ben Gurion, was one of the dynamic and controversial Founding Fathers of the State of Israel. Later, both men served as Prime Minister.

We visited one of the Jewish elders of the city, who led us to important points of interest. "Here, in this synagogue he [Begin] prayed," as the old man pointed to a house of worship, and pointing to another building, "and in that house he was born."

"Do you know why Menachem Begin spent the last years of his life in seclusion?" we asked. And we received a quick answer. "Because that is the custom of the place. Begin learned this from the Kotzker Rebbe, and adopted that style from him. If you feel ill at ease with yourself [in the case of Begin it was the Lebanon war], you enter your own home as a type of house arrest, which then becomes a symbol of depression.

"That indeed was the message he picked up from the Kotzker," continued the old Jew. "To both the Kotzker and Menachem Begin, time was almost irrelevant. What was important was the content of their lives." Thus we came full circle in 200 years, from the illustrious spiritual leader, Rabbi Menachem Mendl of Kotzk, in a small, isolated village, to the former leader of the State of Israel, Menachem Begin. The wisdom of the Kotzker, as fresh today as it was when first passed on to the Gur Chassidic sect. This is one of the largest Chassidic sects in the world today, with tens of thousands of adherents in Israel and throughout the world. Following in the way of the Kotzker Rebbe, Gur is less experience-oriented, and more intellectually inclined than most other Chassidic sects.

Similar stories could be told about the poet Abba Kovner as well as Prime Minister Yitzhak Rabin. Rabin, for example, insisted on reciting the *Kaddish* in his visit to concentration camps in Germany.

The conversation turned to our principal interest. "How about *Kaddish*?" we inquired. "What does Rabbi Mendl have to say about this prayer?" "It would appear," was the reply, "that he regarded it as the yearning of the Jewish heart."

The Kotzker Rebbe evidently felt that the *Kaddish* prayer brought the presence of God into the life of the simple Jew. The Kotzker explained the Biblical phrase, "holy people" to mean that your **holiness** must be **human**. In other words, the spirit of God must descend into the life of the simple Jew, in his daily life.

We have already observed that the *Kaddish* reflects pain, but not death. It offers somewhat of an explanation for why the good suffer, whether it be in the Sho'ah, the wars of Israel, the death of children in terrorist attacks, or disease. The *Kaddish* has a certain mystical (one might almost say "magical") power, a type of invisible bond among Jews, no matter how far one is removed from other Jews, Jewish tradition, and God. That is why we will often find that Jews who say they are cultural but not religious Jews will find a head covering, if nothing more than a handkerchief, when they hear the *Kaddish* recited. The only other prayer that approaches the *Kaddish* in importance among all Jews is the *Shema*, the daily assertion of monotheism.

As noted earlier, the *Kaddish* is in Aramaic, and there are some who maintain that any effort to recite it in translation in any other language—even in Hebrew—will result in diminishing its mystique and "flavor," and it is thus preferable to leave it untouched.

The writer Adam Baruch, who followed in the footsteps of the Kotzker Rebbe and sought to find the inner kernel of what keeps one Jewish, claims that any such a translation will leave the *Kaddish* mortally wounded, because there is a subconscious layer of awareness by Jews of the *Kaddish*, and that will be destroyed if the *Kaddish* is recited in any other language. It is interesting to remember the presence of Baruch at the grave of the Kotzker in faraway Poland, and to note how he brought a *Kaddish*, to Tel Aviv, as if uttered by the Kotzker himself.

Another aspect of Kotzk, set forth by Adam Baruch:[56] He notes that he was fortunate in establishing a prayer quorum of the Komarno Chassidic sect in Jaffa. Many people believe that the Komarno Rebbe was the truest exponent of the views and ways of the Ba'al Shem Tov, the founding spirit of Chassidism.

Here is yet another *Kaddish* story: When the Ba'al Shem Tov's first wife, Channah, died, he asked one of his disciples to say *Kaddish* for her. He promised the man who recited the *Kaddish*, who had a number of daughters but no son, that he would finally be blessed with a son. And so it came to pass.

· 11 ·

PROPHETS, MYSTICISM, AND KADDISH

OUR JOURNEY NOW took us from Poland to Amsterdam. Here, we met with Yitzchak Sonnenschein, whose grandfather, Rabbi Undervizer,[57] was one of the prominent rabbis of the community between the two World Wars.

Sonnenschein guided us to the famous Portuguese Synagogue, across from the Museum of Jewish History. The Museum itself is located in what were once four Ashkenazi synagogues. We followed a canal that bisects the town, to the Holland Theater, where Jews were assembled before being sent to the death camps. A small museum is there, not far from the home of Baruch Spinoza, the nonconformist philosopher who was rejected by the Jewish community because he had the audacity to question certain basic dogmas and beliefs. In fact, many of our ideas about the *Kaddish* were inspired by Spinoza.

Next, we went sightseeing along the Amstel River, near a town called Oudkerk, where there is an old Jewish cemetery. On one of the gravestones was a skull and crossbones.

"What is this?" we asked.

"Well," came the answer, "the man buried here was a Moroccan Jew, and an official pirate in the service of the monarchy. He and his men robbed ships traveling between Holland and Morocco. That is why the tombstone is carved with the Hebrew word *chaver* [comrade] spelled out in Roman letters."

We find the duality of the Dutch hard to understand. On the one hand, this nation has produced many heroes who, often risking their own lives, extended their hand to the persecuted Jews during World War II. At the same time, many Dutch citizens collaborated with the Nazis, and handed over masses of Jews to the Nazis, including Anne Frank and her family.

This duality continues to exist. The extreme right wing of the political parties are violently Jew-haters as well as haters of the million or more foreigners, mostly from Morocco, Algeria, and Turkey, who live in the country.

Sonnenschein then took us to the Biblioteka Rosenthalia, a rare collection of Jewish and Hebrew books within the university. He pointed us to one of these, which discusses the mystical and mysterious nature of death in Jewish thought.

According to Jewish belief, in the World to Come, death will be abolished, one of the signs of the ultimate redemption. In Isaiah 26:19, we read of the revival of the dead: "*Your dead shall live; the dead bodies shall arise—awake and sing, you that dwell in the dust—for your dew is as the dew of light, and the earth shall bring to life the shades."*

Then we have the vision of the dry bones in Ezekiel 37:1–14: *"Thus says the Lord to these bones: 'Behold, I will cause breath to enter into you, and you shall live.'"* And in Daniel 12:2, we read, *"Many of those that sleep in the dust of the earth shall awake, some to everlasting life, and some to reproaches and everlasting abhorrence."* We see that in Daniel, the revival of the dead is linked to reward and punishment. All the mysticism involved in death allowed imagination to take flight, and in Hebrew literature we find accounts of the dead returning to life or speaking among themselves.

There is a *midrash* that tells of Rabbi Yehudah the *Nasi,* who, after his death, would return to his home each Friday afternoon before sunset and instruct members of his household to light his candle in his place and to make his bed ready. (Tractate *Ketubot* 103). He only stopped appearing out of respect for the other sages.

We are told (Tractate *Berachot* 18) that Rabbi Zeira left a sum of money with a woman who was the local innkeeper where he lived, and then went to study Torah. When he returned, he found that the innkeeper had died and had already been buried. He went to the innkeeper's grave and asked her where the money was, and she answered: "It is hidden in the hinge of the front door, where the door turns."

A similar story is told about the father of Shmuel, who had been given money by some orphans for safekeeping. When the father died, Shmuel did not know where the money was. He went to his father's grave and asked where the money was, and his father told him.

We then went to the Anne Frank House. While her story is well known and her death a worldwide legend, the question remains whether or not it leaves us with any philosophical message. Perhaps it does.

We believe no death can occur without causing the relatives of the deceased to slow down and think, to take stock, and to draw conclusions for the future. Every death means that we have to reconsider: Why? How? What does this say to me?

Whenever we are confronted by death, we are forced to ask ourselves basic, existential questions. One is forced to think about the nature of life, man's purpose in the world, and the aim of our existence. After the death of a loved one, a person cannot just go back to the pursuit of material gains without some self-examination. One is now forced to confront basic questions and eternal answers. One's previous values are suddenly shaky and one seeks answers: "What have I done until now? Have I only sought out the pleasures in life, and nothing else?"

In the Bible, the first deaths, of Adam and Eve, occurred because they disobeyed God's command. When instructed not to eat from the Tree of Knowledge, good and evil (Genesis 2:17), "*For on the day you eat from it, you shall surely die.*" One of the great commentators, *Sforno*, states that in this verse God cautioned his first creatures to prepare for the day of their death, as in all generations after them.

According to Jewish tradition, it was the sin of Adam and Eve that brought death to the world; and from that time on there was no escape (Genesis 3:19), "*For dust you are, and to dust you will return.*"

Death takes an even more prominent role in the shaping of humans—when the very first murder took place. Cain killed his brother Abel and thereby became a murderer, signaling that it is possible for one man to kill another.

The Bible is full of stories of various types of deaths,[58] from which we are to learn lessons: Enoch dies prematurely, before his time (Genesis 5:23), "*And he was not, because the Lord took him.*" We also have an important lesson from the death of Abraham: Abraham's death at a ripe old age, makes his life come full circle: "*You will come to your father's house in peace; you will be buried at a ripe old age.*" This is a type of model for the classic Jewish way to part from the world, peacefully: "*Abraham died at a ripe old age, old and satisfied with days, and he was gathered to his people.*"

Anna Frank did not live to a ripe old age, nor was her death a tranquil one. But thanks to her *Diary* she is the epitome of the female Jewish martyr who died in the most terrible pogrom of all—the Sho'ah. There is a typical Chassidic legend regarding departure from this world. A few days before his death, on *Shabbat Ha'Gadol*, the so-called "Great Sabbath," the Sabbath just before Pesach, Rebbe Moshe of Kobrin kept repeating the verse, "Let my soul praise the Lord." He added quietly, "Ah, my soul, in which world will you be? Praise the Lord. But what can I ask the Lord? 'I will praise the Lord during my life.'—I beseech the Lord that as long as I remain alive I will be able to praise Him."

On the last day of Passover, before the grace after meals, he spoke at length. Afterwards, he said, "I have nothing more to say. Let us recite the grace." The next day he became ill, and a week later he died. And Rabbi Nachman of Bratslav said: "All the lusts in the world are comparable to rays of light. The person wants to grasp them, but opens his hand and sees that it's empty."

We returned to the Portuguese Synagogue on *Shabbat*. The chanting there still carried an echo of the Spain before the Jews were expelled in 1492, when many found shelter in Holland. By now, of course, the religious melodies also contain elements of the Dutch culture. The Sephardic Jews who escaped Spain for Holland and other Western countries, brought with them their traditional Spanish music.

At the end of the service, the worshippers sang a unique melody for the *Kaddish titkabel*, with the emphasis on the added line, "May the prayers and supplications of the whole House of Israel be accepted by our Father in Heaven, and say, 'Amen.'" These words are derived from a verse in I Kings 8:45, "Hear you in Heaven their prayer and their supplication, and maintain their cause," which the Aramaic translation takes to mean: "May heaven accept our prayers and supplications."

The reason the words "of the whole House of Israel" were added is that we should not have a prayer just for a single congregation, but for the entire Jewish People. The concept of "our Father" is also to be found, in Isaiah 63:16, "For you are our Father." Here the term is amplified, so that one can see that this is no earthly father, by the addition of "in Heaven." This is similar to (Nehemiah 1:5), "I beseech you, O the Lord, the God of Heaven."

The term "Heaven," thus is derived from the verse in *Kings* quoted above, the prayer of King Solomon, whereas "our Father" relates to the nature of our request, for we ask God to listen to our prayers the same way a child asks his father to listen to his requests and is sure that his request will be granted.

· 12 ·

YAHRZEIT AND YIZKOR:
CHRISTIAN ORIGINS?

WE TRAVELED ON to Antwerp, in Belgium. There, we learned little about *Kaddish*, but a great deal about local Jews and Antwerp, which is the center of the world diamond market.

The large number of Chassidim one sees on the streets gives the feeling of a town in pre-war Eastern Europe, but one with a somewhat modern veneer. The diamond industry that grew here resulted in the establishment of a number of Orthodox synagogues, each identified with a specific group (Belz, Gur, Vizhnitz, Lubavich, Satmar, Sephardic).

All of these have their own religious organizations, rabbis, and teachers. In Antwerp, there are kosher restaurants, bookstores selling holy books, and Jewish educational institutions.

One hears much spoken Yiddish, which is often spoken and understood by non-Jews in the sale of diamonds and precious stones. For example, if two sides conclude an oral agreement with the words *mazel ubrocheh*, that is considered a definite sale, even without a signed document of any kind.

And in the middle of the triangle of streets which one might call a ghetto, there is a park used by many Jews on Sabbath afternoons. It is often referred to colloquially as "Cholent Park," a reference to the familiar meat or vegetable stew set on a stove before the onset of the Sabbath and allowed to cook slowly without the touch of a hand in order to avoid the "labor" of cooking on a holy day.[59]

The Jews of Belgium, even those in Brussels, do not bury their dead inside the country's borders. This is because Belgian laws say a cemetery land can be reclaimed for other uses after one hundred years have passed. This means the ground can be plowed up, the bones of the dead removed, and the land used for other purposes.

Holland doesn't have this provision, so the Jews of Belgium bury their dead there. Yossi Shuldiener, a diamond merchant, the leader of the Jewish community in Antwerp, tells us of a case, where a certain country did not guarantee that its cemeteries would not be uprooted. There, too, the Jews buried their dead in a neighboring country. When the Jews realized that coffins could be transported across the borders without any problem, they began placing bags of diamonds and other precious jewels inside the coffins, along with the body. Thus they were able to smuggle precious stones through the border to sell them in a neighboring country at a handsome profit—some of which was used as a "tip" to a border guard to guarantee the success of the operation.

The story goes that it didn't take long until someone thought of an even more brazen method: Why wait for someone to die before putting items in a coffin? Why not simply stage a funeral, without a body, but with a coffin full of contraband? This, too, worked, as long as certain border guards were in on the deal and got their "commission" for looking the other way.

One day, however, a strange guard was on duty when such a mock "funeral" came through. He observed a large delegation of "mourning" Jews coming from the border checkpoint, carrying a coffin. He was puzzled by the fact that *not a single person was crying*. Instead they were laughing and chatting.

The guard halted the procession and ordered that the coffin be opened. After much resistance and pleading, the group saw that the guard couldn't be moved. He lifted the coffin lid to reveal all the valuable contraband. "All of you are going to prison!" he shouted, brandishing his rifle. Only then did the Jews really start weeping and wailing but it was too late, and a heavy price was paid for their laughter and happy conversation at the wrong time.

The two of us remained in Antwerp for the festival of *Shavu'ot*. We heard a unique and lovely chanting of *Yizkor*, the prayer recited on the anniversary of a death.

Does *Yizkor*, a prayer like *Kaddish*, owe its existence to the pogroms against the Jews in the Middle Ages? The *Yizkor* tradition is to call out the names of those who died in the past year and to pledge charity in their memory.[60] This custom is observed by all Jewish communities on *Yom Kippur*.

The Ashkenazi communities add three other days upon which *Yizkor*[61] is recited: the last day of Passover, *Shavu'ot* (in Israel this is a one-day festival; outside Israel it is said on the second day); and *Shemini Atzeret* (the day after the seven days of *Sukkot*). The concept behind this is that by giving charity in memory of a departed person, the deeds of the living are linked to all the good deeds of the dead, which, in turn, can help the souls of the departed. There were communities that would read aloud the names of all the departed who had relatives of those alive, and communities that kept written records of all who had died. The names of everyone in the community who had died, even if years before ago, were then read.

It is a custom among Ashkenazi Jews that those who have both parents alive leave the synagogue during *Yizkor*. Among reasons given for this unusual custom is that, since non-mourners do not say *Kaddish*, without them all those in the building would be praying. Among Ashkenazim, *Yizkor* has often occupied a central place, to the extent that people who do not generally attend the synagogue will often do so on those days on which *Yizkor* is said.

Yizkor and *Yarhzeit* come from the same source. Since that period of time, when Jews had no means to express and ventilate their grief; they needed a means to memorialize their dead. Thus one can see how the ritual of *Kaddish*, *Yatom*, and *Yarhzeit* were inspired from Christian rituals. Obviously, the Christian rituals were seen as a means for the Christians to relieve their grief. Therefore, it is possible to assume that the Jewish ritual was inspired, by the Christians. One must take note astonishingly that two of the most fundamental prayers in Judaism, *Kaddish* and *Av ha'rachamin* were borrowed and emulated from Christian ritual.

Early Christianity's dogma is based on the belief that physical death is inevitable because we are merely human.

Through union with Jesus and the Christian Church, believers become participants in the messianic resurrection and the victory over death, a victory that will become all-embracing with the resurrection of the dead at the End of Days. This is to say, a spiritual victory that invites the mourners' joy. This was the stand of early Christianity which later replaced the joyous acceptance with mourning over the dead; the customary practice of wearing white clothes was replaced with the wearing of black ones, and the prayers for the deceased dealt with redeeming their souls from the punishment of Hell. This necessitated a confession of the moribund performed by a priest. The ritual includes also spraying holy water and offering incense. In the last 40 years, Christians have returned to a sense that funerals are a time for hopefulness and faith. The threat of Hell is no longer a part of the liturgy.

Some Christians made a habit of cremating the body, a custom that aroused a great dispute in the Church. The ritual ceremony of laying the dead to their final rest includes, in addition to the main text, various customs like dressing the deceased in their best clothes and laying them in a coffin to be presented to all co-mourners.

The Christian ceremony of burial often uses a text taken from Psalms 23: *The Lord is my Shepherd; I shall not want. He maketh me to lie down in green pasture. He leads me beside the still waters, He restores my soul. He leadeth me in the paths of righteousness for His name's sake. Yea, though I walk through the valley of the shadow of death I will fear no evil because Thou art with me; Thy rod and Thy staff they comfort me.* The priest then recites a prayer constituting of an absolution to the deceased soul.

The Jews did not have such a ritual but with time and necessity they adopted the idea of having one and furnished it with a different text—the text of the *Kaddish*. The *Kaddish*, like Psalms: 23, sharpens the recognition that the Lord created a world to his pleasing, a world whose procedures we do not thoroughly understand. But this is the nature and order of things as determined by the Providence and it is for the best.

In the Jewish ritual of burial the deceased is dressed in simple and straight white linen shrouds having no pockets. This is another trait of the social view of Judaism: everybody will be buried in the same clothes whether rich or poor, as opposed to the Christians who dress their dead in their "best" clothes or of the family's choosing.

Christians also sometimes put in the coffin a symbolic object of the deceased life, or of social or geographic environment. Loved ones might place tokens in the coffin, but it is not part of the ritual or required. These objects may be present in the coffin during the wake (viewing of the deceased) but would be removed for the funeral. Judaism forbids placing in the tomb any object: a man passes away clean and pure, free of any physical assets (this is why shrouds have no pockets). His hands too are spread open to show he is taking nothing with him to a world of total goodness. From now on only his soul is important.

And another ritual difference between Jews and Christians: The latter bury their dead in a coffin. The Jews do not do so unless it is an important rabbi or a notable or in cases of horrible damage to the body. Judaism grasps that "from dust thou art and unto dust shalt thou return" (Genesis: 3, 19), therefore no need for a coffin. (The coffin, too, serves as a criterion to the richness of the deceased or his family and therefore it is superfluous since all men are equal before God when arriving unto his kingdom.) The shrouds are wrapped in a *talith*—the very Jewish symbol—which is removed before the actual burial.

· 13 ·

JUDAISM AND THE IDEA OF DEATH

$\mathcal{F}$ROM ANTWERP WE flew to Budapest, the capital of Hungary. Our taxi from the airport took us past a string of luxury hotels in the hills of Buda, then down to the lower city, across the beautiful Danube, and through various alleys to the Jewish quarter. In it, there are two synagogues, the "Kazinczy," so called because of the street on which they were built, along with the Great Synagogue of the Neolog (Reform) community on Dohány Street.

With a seating capacity of 3,000, the Great Synagogue of the Neolog is the largest synagogue in Europe and the second-largest in the world. Only Temple Emmanuel on New York's Fifth Avenue is larger.

The Great Synagogue is not only one of the largest, but one of the most beautiful. We were moved by a metal sculpture shaped like an olive tree, on which each leaf is inscribed with the name of a Hungarian Jew killed by the Nazis in the last year of the Sho'ah.

There is still controversy surrounding those events. A Slovakian Jew named Rudi Vrba was a registrar at Auschwitz. He and a companion were the first two ever to successfully escape. In his book, *I Escaped from Auschwitz* (Barricade Books) he tells how he fled to Budapest and alerted Rudolf Kastner, the leader of the Jewish community, to the Nazi plan to murder 400,000 Hungarian Jews.

Satisfied that by telling what he knew to Kastner he had successfully warned the community, Rudi Vrba went into hiding in what was then Czechoslovakia. But Kastner had other ideas. He went directly to Adolf Eichmann and made a deal whereby he would keep silent in return for which his family and about 1,100 young Jewish men would be allowed to travel to Palestine via Switzerland.

The Jew had betrayed his fellow Jews.

Years later someone wrote some harsh truths about Kastner, who was living in Israel, and Kastner sued for libel. During the trial, Kastner was assassinated in the street.

Going back, at least two hundred thousand Hungarian Jews, who might have resisted if they had known their destination was the gas oven of Treblinka, went innocently to their deaths.

Raul Hilberg in his monumental book, *The Destruction of European Jews*, makes this interesting observation. Where Jews were taken from communities where they depended on a strong Rabbi or Jewish leader, they went without resistance.

But Jews who came from areas where there was no strong leader tended to resist, breaking out of their cattle cars and attacking their guards. Rudi Vrba died in 2006. His newspaper obituaries credited him with saving the lives of 200,000 Hungarian Jews.

It was here in Budapest too that the drama of Channah Senesh[62] was played to its bitter conclusion. Senesh had been parachuted into Hungary during World War II to help the Jews there. She was caught by the Nazis and brutally tortured before being killed. Here also the waters of the Blue Danube were said to have turned red from the blood of the thousands of Jews who were chained and thrown into the water alive by the Iron Cross (the Hungarian Nazis), who tried to outdo the Germans in their passion to slaughter Jews.

Budapest was also where Raoul Wallenberg, an angel on earth, worked to keep thousands of Jews out of the hands of the Nazis.

The official ledger of the Burial Society of Budapest Jewry of 1860 discusses the sanctity of life and lists the customs and practices incumbent upon a mourner. These were intended to decrease the pain one felt after the death of a loved one. All of this was in keeping with the way Rabbi Elimelech of Lizhensk described death: as moving from one residence to another, except that a wise person will choose a better one—the Garden of Eden—than the one he inhabits at present.

It is perhaps appropriate at this point to digress from our study of the lore of *Kaddish* to a commentary on death in general, a subject we tend to avoid and one which is almost taboo among some people.

There is no more difficult a time for an individual than

after the loss of a close relative. There is a feeling of shock, of loss, of a vacuum that has suddenly been created and which can never be filled. Beyond words is the awareness that there can be no replacement for the loved one. All of these feelings result in a trauma that burns deeply into one's soul. But it is generally agreed among most behavioral scientists that the Jewish approach to death and mourning is of major value in dealing with such trauma, and not only in terms of belief and faith.

According to Jewish belief, the basic premise is that while the body is indeed buried, the soul remains, and the deceased moves from the material world to another world, the World to Come, "a world which is solely good." In other words, leaving this world is not the end of one's existence. Skeptics point out that the soul doesn't have memory, but true believers ignore reason in favor of faith. They believe there is life for the human soul outside its human body.

When Abraham died, Genesis 25:8 tells us, "he was gathered to his people," namely that his soul joined the souls of other departed. As Rabbi Akiva put it, "This world is like an entrance hall to the World to Come. Prepare yourself in the entrance hall so that you may enter the main hall."

Jewish belief stresses that the body and soul are two separate entities, which are united only as long as the person is alive. When one dies, the soul ascends for all eternity. "Is this nothing but a kind of psychotherapy?" we wonder. "Is this a way to calm the bereaved, to lessen their burden?"

The belief in the survival of the soul after death as well as the belief in the revival of the dead, require the mourner to emerge from the shock involved in the loss, to gradually come to terms with that loss and to go through a mourning process. This will eventually free him or her from deep depression and enable a return to normal life. After all, even though the loved one has died, the soul will survive forever.

In traditional Jewish belief, one's soul is entrusted to one's body throughout life, and when the time comes for the soul to depart from the world, it returns to its Maker.[63] This is what Job has declared: (Job 1:21): "The Lord has given; the Lord has taken away; may the name of the Lord be blessed."

Some wonder, "Is that just a fatalistic comment, based on a deterministic view and belief in fate as the ultimate determiner?" "No," others reply. "On the contrary: it is this sentiment which exemplifies the optimism of the Jewish people in its most trying moments, and the absolute faith of the individual in God. It leads Job to express the hope that when the Revival of the Dead takes place, he will be resurrected. One of the aspects of our ultimate redemption will be the abolition of death. As we find in Isaiah 25:8, "He will swallow up death for ever; the Lord will wipe away tears from all faces; and the disgrace of His people will He take away from all the earth."

The sages of post-Biblical times believed in the survival of the soul after death. They used the phrase in Temple observances "from the world to the world," to emphasize that there are two worlds, the world we inhabit and the World to Come.

It is from such a vantage point that one can understand Judaism's view of death. Judaism sanctifies life, and considers each life as the equivalent of the entire world. It tells us (*Sanhedrin* 37), "If one destroys a single person it is as if he had destroyed the entire world, and one who keeps a single person alive as if he had kept the entire world alive." A person must do everything to save another's life.

In addition, one must keep harmful objects away from people, in order to avoid any chance of injury or death. (Deuteronomy 22:8): "You shall not place any blood [i.e., any item which might cause injury or death] in your home." To God, the sanctity of life is paramount, regardless of religion or race. Thus we are told (Tractate *Megillah* 10) that when the Egyptians pursued the Children of Israel, who had just fled from Egypt, and the Egyptians were drowned in the waters of the Sea of Reeds, the angels wished to sing praises of God for rescuing the Children of Israel, but God said to them: "My creatures are drowning in the sea and you wish to recite praise?"

Saving a human life takes precedence over all the other commandments. Thus, one may violate the Sabbath to save a human life. As the Talmud tells us (*Yoma* 85), "Violate one Sabbath, in order to [be able to] observe many Sabbaths" [in the future]. The logical conclusion from this—and that, indeed, is Jewish law—is that one may only violate the Sabbath if one may thereby save a human life.

One may not, however violate it for someone already dead. As our Sages tell us, "For a live day-old child, one may violate the Sabbath, but one may not violate the Sabbath for King David once he is dead."

Two stories about the last minutes on earth of saintly men reveal a clearer perception of the Jewish way of death.[64]

Rabbi Meir of Premishlan, d. 5630 (1870), prepared for his death in great detail. With a clear and very incisive mind, he sent letters to various Chassidic rabbis asking them to send him "endorsements" before his death. On the last Thursday of his life, he told the Chassidim who were present: "Anyone who does not want to spoil the coming Sabbath should go home now." And indeed, that Sabbath he died, returning his soul to his Maker in purity.

Another story: When Rabbi Moshe of Sambor's illness became critically severe and he was close to death, he asked his fellow Chassidim to carry him into the study hall and to lay him down with his feet pointing toward the door. When this was done, he called the Chassid who was in charge of singing and asked him to sing the melody with the words (Psalms 104:33), "I will sing to the Lord as long as I live; I will sing praise to my God while I have any breath," but as loud as possible to relieve some of his pain.

The townspeople heard the singing and hurried into the study hall. The singer sang on, tears streaming down his cheeks. Rabbi Moshe's son, Rabbi Michel, finally said, "Father, we simply don't have the strength to cry any more. Let us bring you to your room." His father became angry at him and said: "Why don't you let me repent?" So they continued to sing until his soul departed.

We strolled along the quay of the Danube River, where we were joined by a local Jew who described the past and present of the Hungarian Jewish community. First there was the anti-Semitism of the 19th century. This culminated in the blood libel of Tiszaeszlar in 1882 and the White Terror of the years between the two World Wars, in which many Jews were killed.

All of this was evidently but a prologue to World War II, when more than 200,000 Hungarian Jews were murdered by the Germans. We wondered, with our companion, how one can reconcile this with the Torah which is "a Torah of Life." It is the customs of mourning that could contain an answer to the question.

In general, the Torah is indeed "a Torah of life." Thus, one of the great rabbis of the Talmud, Shmuel, commenting on the verse (Leviticus 18:5), "You shall therefore keep My statutes, and My ordinances, which if a man does, he shall live by them: I am the Lord," says: "He shall live by them and not die by them."

It is God, Creator of the world, who wants man to live. It is He who gives life and He who takes life, and He who sanctifies life. Just as life is sanctified, its antithesis, death, is profane, and anyone coming in contact with a dead person must be purified. Thus we see that in Jewish life, death is below life in the hierarchy. With this approach to death and mourning, the Torah commands the Jew: Do not adopt the customs of the non-Jews in mourning. You are not to overemphasize the signs of mourning. The human mechanism gradually returns the mourner to normal life and Jewish law does the same. That is why Jewish law does not allow one to mourn excessively.

On the one hand, anyone who does not mourn for a departed close relative is cruel, while on the other we are told (Jeremiah 22:10): "Weep you not for the dead, neither bemoan him." One does not weep excessively for the dead. One does not gash the skin or tear out one's hair as a sign of mourning, as was done in ancient times.

Jewish law sets the first three days after a death for weeping, the first seven for eulogizing, and the first thirty days for not wearing new clothing, cutting one's hair, or shaving. Beyond that point, God sets up guidelines (*Mo'ed Katan 27*): "You cannot be more merciful than I—do not show more mercy than I do."

There may be the origin of the saying: Do not be more merciful than the Creator Himself.[65]

· 14 ·

THE PSYCHOLOGICAL DYNAMIC TO DEATH IN JUDAISM

WE MADE A major leap, from Europe to the border between Europe and Asia. We went to Istanbul, Turkey, with its Bosporus Strait and minarets, mosques with luxury cars lined up, and fancy stores.

Turkey is a country that seems to have fallen between the cracks, with a general preference for the West, yet with a contingent of extreme fundamentalists who wish a return it to pristine Islam. There are even Muslim clerics who wish to bring the caliphate back to Turkey and to the entire Muslim world. Without doubt, secularism and its fellow-traveler, Western imperialism, are to them the root of every evil in the world.

The twin bombings of synagogues in Istanbul on November 15, 2003, in which 23 people were killed, were a follow-up to a bombing in one of these same synagogues in 1986, in which 22 people were killed. These were followed by attacks on the British consulate and other British targets, making Istanbul into "Israel II," where the Turks experienced for the first time what Israel has been suffering for decades. The street on which the twice bombed Neveh Shalom synagogue is located, is a narrow one-way street leading to the Galata Tower. One might develop a interesting theory about the mobilization of world Jewry, especially as it occurred in Israel, following the attacks in Turkey. It is here one can see the beginning of an attempt to have Israel, the Jews of Turkey, and of the United States, France, and Britain realize that they share a common world-wide enemy, even though they may not share a common culture or language.

Every event in the Jewish world brings an immediate response by Israel, as if Israel had a great deal in common with the Diaspora communities throughout the world. In other words, it is the negative tie which unifies all.

The Israeli Jew lives in a closed country. He has existential and survival fears, and he seeks a display of strength from his brothers. The slaughter in Istanbul, among which a number of the victims were Jews, accentuated the sense of failure in Jewish eyes. After the attack in November 2003, most of whose victims were Muslims, the Muslim neighbors of the synagogues said that they would prefer to have the Jewish synagogues "outside the city center . . . because the synagogues pose too great a danger."

We listen to the elders of the Jewish community and are impressed with their ancient ties to the city. The Jews came here from Spain in 1492, after having been expelled by the rabidly anti-Semitic Ferdinand and Isabella. The injustice of their actions was heightened by the contrary tolerance with which they were greeted by the Ottoman sultan, Bayezid II.[66]

To this day, one can hear the Jews of the second synagogue which was attacked, the Neveh Shalom synagogue, speak among themselves an ancient form of Spanish, passed down from their parents. The wealthy Jews who had lived in the center of the city have moved to outlying suburbs. There are, though, still a few thousand Jews who still live near the synagogue. At the center of this neighborhood is a small bakery, where one can obtain kosher baked goods.

Many Jews trade in the large bazaar of Istanbul. Young Jewish merchants admit that in spite of the glorious history of the Jews in the city, it is very difficult to look to the future there with equanimity. They are nevertheless optimistic, and one says: "We've been here for 500 years and will continue to live here." Across the counter from him is an Israeli customer, a wealthy tourist who is considered an excellent customer.

"Are suffering and death a catharsis which purifies and refines one?" We believe that this is an accepted belief in Jewish life. The world evidently cannot survive without suffering, and suffering is an inseparable part of it. Even the study of Torah, an enjoyable experience in itself, is considered of inestimably greater value if carried out in spite of suffering. Thus, our sages tell us (*Horayot* 11), "The Torah can only survive within one who 'kills himself' (i.e., shows total dedication) for it."

We wonder: "Doesn't death, evil, and pain create a contradiction to one's daily routine, to one's pleasures, to one's hedonistic pursuits, when opposed to major crises in one's life, death being one of these?"

There is no doubt that an event such as the synagogue explosion in Turkey forces one to "break the mold" and to grapple with basic questions. It means bringing to the fore concerns which have often been suppressed deeply. This idea is expressed succinctly in the words of R. Menachem Mendl of Kotzk,[67] who believed that suffering is the only thing which can arouse us to begin thinking of our place in the world.

We are told in Psalms 119:71, *It is good for me that I have been afflicted, in order that I might learn Your statutes.* It is the suffering of doubt, the pain of uncertainty, which is the only remedy separating death from life, and it is this which will bring about truth; only then will the enveloping darkness disappear, leaving in its place a great light.

Rebbe Menachem Mendl said: "Man was created in order to bore into the depths of the heavens." What he meant is that throughout one's life one has to be engaged in soul-searching, to strive to find the truth, to live in an atmosphere of evil and suffering, yet, within all of this to be able to soar from the very depths to the very heights: "One of my feet is in the Seventh Heaven, while the other is in the deepest of depths," said the rabbi.

Thus, a person may even question the very existence of God, the same God who took one's dear one, yet ultimately arrive at the truth, and faith in the justice of the Creator.

Evil and death are thus necessary ingredients in our lives because they serve to make us more understanding. They are not a punishment or a decree against us, but are part of the order of Creation. The questions which arise when one has lost a loved one often relate to the fact that God seems to have "hidden His face."

The mourner asks: "Why this particular person now? Why did he suffer? After all, he was such a good person, a true believer ..."

There is an answer to all of these questions: Death is part of the natural order of things. As Rabbi Meir put it, death is one of the set parameters of life in the world, and is therefore not a punishment. Thus, on the verse, "*Behold, it was very good*" (in Hebrew: *tov me'od*), Rabbi Meir expounded, "*tov mavet*"—death is good.

We wonder how it is that Jewish philosophy can determine categorically, as in Ecclesiastes 7:2, that "*It is better to go to the house of mourning, than to go to the house of feasting, for that is the end of all men, and the living will take it to his heart.*"

When people die, do they leave a legacy for the living? Will this prod them to repent, the byproduct which will be the forgiveness of their sins? We quote Rabbi Yishmael, who said: "If a person carried out an act which leads to a Desecration of Heaven ... repentance and Yom Kippur atone for a third [of the sin], suffering atones for [another] third, and one's death cleanses one's suffering" (*Tosefta Yoma* 4:6). Rabbi Yehudah the Exilarch also declared, "One's death serves to atone" (*Mekhilta d'Rabbi Yishmael*).

We continued our examination of Jewish religious values, particularly with respect to concepts of death and life, inspired by the Talmud itself and an idea we had considered earlier outside the Great Mosque in Istanbul. The Talmud raises the question whether it was better that Man was created, or that Man was never created.

The Talmud's conclusion appears at first glance to be absurd: "In the end they decided that it would have been better had Man not been created, but now that he has been created, he should constantly examine his actions" (*Eiruvin* 13). This is a definitive conclusion: it would have been better for us not to have been created, but since we have no choice in the matter and were created anyway, it is clear that our attitude to life cannot be encapsulated in "eat and drink, for tomorrow we die."

One does not come to the world with the idea expressed in Genesis 25:32, *"I am at the point of dying; and what value does the birthright have for me?"* i.e., that one's existence is of no consequence. To the contrary, once in the world, one must examine one's ways and sanctify one's life.

During the Ten Days of Repentance, from Rosh Hashanah to Yom Kippur, we beseech God, "Remember us for life, O King who desires life," and "Inscribe us in the Book of Life." Thus we indicate clearly that life itself has great value, and is not merely a chance configuration of physical matter which evolved into a human being. Only after we have asked God for life do we move to secondary requests: earning a living, health, peace. Without life, all the rest are worthless.

When we speak of an individual having had a "length of days," we are not talking about a person who simply lived to a ripe old age, but rather about one who used his hours on this earth wisely and whose quality of life made each day one of value, one filled with spiritual challenges and rewarding achievements. Days of that kind impart meaning to one's life.

It is important to strive to live such a life. It is in the hope that each person will try to live up to that ideal that the

Torah stresses the need to have doctors "who will heal" one. It is thus not surprising that so many of the great rabbis, especially those in Spain, were also medical doctors.

Judaism's attitude is in Deuteronomy 30:19, "*Choose Life.*" This is in direct opposition to what we read in Ecclesiastes 2:17, "*I hate life.*" Our lives need to be devoted to spiritual matters, as *Ba'al Haturim,* the great master of Jewish numerology points out. He notes that in the Torah phrase, "*Choose life,*" the word used in Hebrew for life, "*bechaim,*" has a numerical value of 70. Similarly, in the verse (Psalms 25:14), "*The secret of the Lord is with those that fear Him,*" the word *sod* ("secret" in the verse) also has a numerical value of 70. And there are two other "seventies." Man's life span is listed as 70, as are the 70 different facets of Torah study. Thus, we see that the secret of living a full life is by choosing "life," and that means a life devoted to the 70 aspects of the Torah.

One might ask: "According to Jewish law, is death supposed to be a means for us, the survivors, to examine our ways?" And there is a Jewish response: "Indeed, it is meant to be a time for soul-searching, for seeking new paths and goals, a better and more meaningful lifestyle. That means one that is both humanitarian and constructive.

Death is not meant to be a destructive force in the survivors' lives but, on the contrary, to be the foundation for moving on into the future. In short, it is meant to tip the scales from a negative to a positive balance. On the one hand, death causes a person to be depressed and melancholy. At the same time it offers that person the opportunity to scale new heights, to turn to the classic lifestyle of traditional Jewish life.

As we came to the close of our geographical search for a

greater understanding of the *Kaddish*, there on the banks of the Bosporus, we felt we had arrived at a point of clarification of some key Judaic concepts about suffering, death, and life.

Suffering and pain are a rude awakening from one's illusions, the feeling of satisfaction, the routines of daily life, and the dulling of one's senses. We can see that one must thank God even when calamity strikes. Even though this is extremely difficult, one must harness all one's resolve to do so.

When our sages say that one is required to thank God for the bad just as one does for the good, it is based on a classic interpretation of the verse in Deuteronomy 6:5, *"You shall love the Lord your God with all your heart and all your might."* The Hebrew words for *all your might* are *bechol me'odecha*, which our sages interpret to mean *"bechol midah she Hu moded lecha"*—that one must love God regardless of whatever burden is imposed on us.

This explains the blessing the Jew recites when he hears evil tidings: "Blessed is the True Judge." Then, at a funeral, one adds: "God gave and God took—may the name of God be blessed." In the same context, Rabbi Meir said: "A person should be accustomed to say, 'Whatever God does is for the best.'"

The Talmud (*Berachot* 60) tells a story to illustrate this. Rabbi Akiva, in his wanderings, arrived at a certain town. He sought an inn for overnight lodging but none was to be had.

"This," he said to himself: "is the will of God; all is for the best." Finally, he found a place to sleep in the nearby fields. He had with him his donkey, a rooster, and one candle. Suddenly, a lion attacked and killed his donkey. A cat grabbed and killed his rooster. The wind blew out his candle.

He refused to be saddened by all these calamities. He continued to believe that whatever God does is for the best. That night, enemy soldiers conducted a surprise attack on the town. They made a captive of every inhabitant.

Later, Rabbi Akiva told his students, "See what I told you? Whatever God did was for the good. Had I found lodging in the town, I too would have been taken captive. If my donkey and rooster would have remained alive, the donkey's braying or the rooster's crowing would have given me away and the soldiers would have found me. The same is true with my candle, which would have led the soldiers to me. Thus you can see that whatever God does is for the good."

In Jewish tradition, the souls of the departed continue to illuminate our lives. The Kabbalah stresses this forcefully in the following way: There is no such thing as a lonely, isolated and lost soul. All souls are linked together in the historical fabric of the Jewish nation, from its founding into eternity.

The Hebrew Bible provides the ultimate insights. In the Book of Job, this classic tragic figure of the Bible undergoes a painful metamorphosis. When he is overcome by suffering, he points an accusatory finger at Heaven and accuses God of torturing him, inflicting suffering without justification, and mistakenly confusing *Iyov*—the Hebrew name for Job—with *Oyeiv*, God's "enemy," as it were.

Our wisest sages tell us (*Bava Batra* 16a) that God does not make mistakes, that things do not happen "by chance." Everything is calculated in Heaven and guided by God: "God said to Job: "I created many hairs on each person's head, and each hair has its own root . . . Now, if I don't confuse one root for another, will I confuse an *Iyov* for an *Oyeiv?*" Judaism demands of Job—both the biblical and the modern one—

including one who has survived the Sho'ah or who has lost relatives on the battlefield, to go on with one's life and trust in God.

In the biblical story, the first deaths, those of Adam and Eve, occurred because the two had disobeyed God's command when instructed not to eat from the Tree of Knowledge (Genesis 2:17), "*For on the day you eat from it, you shall surely die*." One of the great commentators, *Sforno*, states that in this verse God cautioned his first humans to prepare for the day of their death, as should all future generations after them.

According to Jewish tradition, it was the sin of Adam and Eve which brought death to the world; and from that time on there would be no escape (Genesis 3:19), "*For dust you are, and to dust you will return*." Death takes an even more prominent role in the shaping of Man in this world, when the very first murder took place. Cain kills his brother Abel and becomes a murderer, signaling that it is possible for one man to kill another. The Bible is full of stories of types of deaths, from which we are to learn lessons: Enoch dies prematurely, before his time (Genesis 5:23), "*And he was not, because the Lord took him*." We also have an important lesson from the death of Abraham: Abraham's easy death at a ripe old age makes his life come full circle: "*You will come to your father's in peace; you will be buried at a ripe old age*." This is a type of model for the classic Jewish way to part from the world, peacefully: "*Abraham died at a ripe old age, old and satisfied with days, and he was gathered to his people*."[58]

PART TWO

Dark History Provides a Need for Kaddish

How the history of the Crusade period and thereafter relating to Jewish people necessitates the need for prayer and ritual. Kaddish Yatom (Orphan's Kaddish) begins its existence.

In the following chapters, we outline in historical detail pogroms, random killing, blood libel, Black Plague, and various historical persecutions against the Jewish people. This bloody and morbid part of Jewish history laid the foundation for the necessity of creating a prayer or ritual which could structure a mourning process unavailable until this period within Jewish traditions; this is the historical and theological context from which Kaddish became one of the most predominant rituals in Judaism.

It is practiced so regularly and it is so ubiquitous that those reciting the prayer rarely think or inquire about its history or its origination. It is so fundamental and, in a way, habit forming that usually it provokes no thought of the profound Jewish history it represents.

It is a constant reminder of death for them without there being cognizance of its references. This part of the book illuminates to the reader the sources of the prayer and links the mourner forever with his or her forefathers and their suffering and creates a national experience.

These chapters will trace how Jewish text from the Talmud was wedded to Christian custom to yield a timely needed ritual of mourning to alleviate grief & sorrow thrust upon them from the crusades, massacres & persecutions in Western Europe.

What is interesting and fascinating is a ritual that emanated in Germany (Ashkenazi) became a custom in Spain (Sephardic) and was thereafter made a permanent part of halacha.

As we will see in these chapters the profundity of this event will show when the ritual returned to Central Europe it was universally applied as halacha. This is one of the exceptional instances in Jewish practice where one can trace how a ritual custom became Halachic law.

· 15 ·

DID THE CRUSADES GIVE BIRTH TO THE KADDISH FOR THE COMMON MAN VIS-À-VIS THE ELITE?

*T*HE ADVENT OF the 1096 convention in Claremont headed by Pope Urban II led to the formation of an army to purge the Holy Land of its Moslem infidels. On the way, the Christian crusaders attacked Jewish congregations in the Rhine district and killed scores of Jews in Vermaiza (Worms), Magenza (Meinz), Colognia (Cologne), Ashpira (Spire), and the surrounding areas.

There arose a need for the Jewish population, a prayer for the tens of thousands who found their deaths in ravaged communities. The need grew stronger as the Black Plague (14th century) left in its wake fifty million corpses, among whom were millions of Jews.[69]

This combination of atrocity and natural catastrophe gave birth to elegies, poetry, commemorations, fast days, and various mourning symbols, something that allowed the Jews to memorialize the disaster that had befallen them. For example:

> The holy ones killed during the persecutions of the year "Tatnu," 1096 recited elegies. Elazar from Germiza (12th-13th cent.), also known as Elazar the Small, the "pathetic," quoted the following eternal verse of Yehuda Halevy: "Zion, will you not seek the safety of your prisoners?" which was later included in the elegies of Tisha B'Av. Clonimus, the son of Rabbi Yehuda Halevi quotes: "If only my head were a source of water and my eyes a source of liquid, then I would cry all my days and nights for my dead, both young and old."

> Hillel, the son of Jacob from Berna (Bern) (12th cent.), who established on the 20th of the month of Sivan (1171) a fast day commemorating the spilling of the blood in France, wrote: "The faithful of Israel . . . when they were taken to be burnt together they were as joyous as a bride on her way to the marriage canopy. . . . You are beautiful, my wife, you are beautiful. . . ." (added to the atonement prayers of Yom Kippur, Reisen).

> The Jews of Bluash (Blois) were burned at the stake while singing "Let us give praise" and in Orleans the burial day of the fallen was declared a day of mourning and fasting. However, the "Gaon" Rabbi Jacob ben Meir, who wrote: "Greater will this fast day (the 23rd of the month of Kislev) be than the fast day of Gedalia, for it is a day of atonement," was buried without an official, established elegy. When the Talmud was put to the torch

in Paris by the Jewish convert Nicholas Donin, acting under the influence of his Dominican friends in 1239, that day was declared a day of fasting as well. In Germany, the Maharam from Rothenburg wrote, "My nether world is scorched by fire … I will cover myself with a sackcloth of mourning … for the souls of the dead, the fallen, are many." This too in reference to the burning of the Talmud, an elegy which is recited on Tisha B'Av.

The blood libels at the end of the 13th cent., 200 years after the Crusades of Germany, gave birth to this hymn about the atrocities of the period: "With this abominable and blood-stained bread they have plotted their scheme … my lyre mourns and my organ emits sounds of crying."

After the vicious slaughter of 15,000 Virga Jews, Rabbi Shlomo Ibn Virga searched for appropriate words to express the profound loss of life, as did Rabbi Chaim Galipupo (1348) of Aragon who mourned the "Black Death" ("and they brought a deadly poison onto the world"). And so the Jews who drank from the poison cup in Sholshuna, Tzalkuna, and Alsace died from the "curse of the lepers," as it was then referred to.

During these unhappy times the reciting of the *Kaddish* began to take hold and fill the vacuum that had been created due to the untold deaths. This was a slow process; it did not take root immediately.

The *Kaddish*, which gratified a burning need, began being recited partly as a result of the writings of and stories about Rabbi Moshe, Ben Rabbi Elazar HaCohen, and Rav Mordechai Ben Rabbi Hillel. But even without knowledge of any specific promulgator, the *Kaddish* became rooted in the conscience of the people as a deeply spiritual prayer which revitalized them in their time of need.

Religious doubts sprang up in many minds in the face of wholesale death and the *Kaddish* therefore arose from within the tragedy as if to say: We continue to glorify and praise God despite the flowing stream of Jewish blood.

At first it was recited only after the study of Torah. Eventually its use was expanded to serve as a channel to preserve the link between Divine Providence and mortal man below who struggles on even though his whole world has collapsed, whose loved ones have died by sword or fire in the name of God Almighty.

The *Kaddish* continues to be recited in Aramaic to announce and inform that the terrible, secular trials experienced by the people still contain an element of holiness whose essence is expressed. Although the text was available there was no connection between the words and the ritual of the Orphan's *Kaddish* and we have no knowledge of exactly who could be termed the official promulgator or originator of the ritual. There are numerous theories but no definitive answer in the *Kaddish* as it was worded in Babylon, in the language of the "common man." "May His Name be great," the foundation of any *Kaddish*, is a symbol of continued faith in the Creator of the universe despite the slaughter and destruction of this world.

Slowly the *Kaddish* entered into the hearts of man and was used on a daily basis. At first it was recited only for luminaries of the Torah who were killed as a result of the Crusades and Black Plague. This is confirmed in the writings of and stories about Rabbi Shlomo Ben Shimon from Magenza and Colognia, Rav Elazar Ben Rabbi Natan, Rav Ashtori

Ha'Parchi (one of those expelled from France), Marat Rachel, daughter of Rav Itzhak, the son of Rabbi Asher and wife of Rav Yehuda, who martyred herself and her four children, as well as Aba Meri Ben Moshe Don Estruk, who was expelled from France. In addition moreover we have further confirmation in the writings of Rabbi Meir from Rothenburg. The following is a study of the chronology that relates to the *Kaddish* and its relationship to the Rosh and Rabbi Meir.

Following the massacre in Germany, Rosh sought refuge in Spain which at the time was peaceful. Rosh is an acronym for Rabbi Asher ben Yechiel, who was a luminary Talmudic scholar who added his own tosofot *to the Talmud and compiled a* halachic *code. The leader of Spanish Jews, Rashba (acronym for Rabbi Shlomo ben Aderet), invited Rosh to Barcelona and supported his appointment as Chief Rabbi of Toledo.*

After Rashba's death, Rosh became the leader of Spanish Jewry. He was the most important link between Sephardic scholarship and Ashkenazim tradition inherited by him personally from Rabbi Meir of Rothenburg.

The Rosh's son, Jacob, known for compilation of a halachic *code in four volumes known as* ar ba's turim, *got to be renowned as the author* Ba'al Ha'turim. *In reference to laws of mourning, he specifically writes about* Kaddish *and aims to bring to conclusion a very intense Ashkenazi debate.*

There was a dispute with respect to the reciting of Kaddish between various cities (e.g., Worms, Meinz) on whether to say the Kaddish on festive holidays (e.g., first of the month, Rosh Chodesh,

Purim, and Hanukah) or not. The debate whether it be recited on
Yom Tov has been going on ever since the Geonic times, but after
the Crusades, it intensified. Among the participants in the debate,
one may find Rashi's school, the Maharam, the Rosh in Ashkenaz,
as well as the Nachmonides in Spain.

In this great Talmudic debate it seems that Rabbi Jacob, son
of Rosh, follows Rashi and his own father, the Rosh, in decid-
ing that Kaddish should be recited on all holidays in the Dias-
pora's second days.

Rabbi Joseph Karo, a Sephardic Jew of Spanish origin resid-
ing in Palestine, who authored the famous code of Jewish law,
Shulhan A'ruch, *was the first to refer to laws of mourning and*
relate to the Kaddish Yatom *as such. In his law of mourning,*
while recognizing various local customs, he transformed them
into Halacha. The principle of Kaddish *is thereby universalized,*
allowing for the diversity of practice.

Karo's halachic judgment became rapidly accepted through-
out the Jewish world. It was the Rama (acronym for Rabbi
Moses Iserles) who added editorial comments to the Shulhan
A'ruch *to make it acceptable to Ashkenazi Jews.* Kaddish
thereby became an all inclusive prayer.

This theory derives from Tractate Kallah, *which basically*
states that one may look upon this mitzvah like a medical treat-
ment or other necessary assistance which may be needed for the
parents by a third party. It is derived from the sense of caring one
should give to his or her parents. Thus there is thought that the
hiring of a Kaddish *reciter resembles a caregiver and thus this*
mitzvah can be achieved and correctly halachically observed.

Moreover, one should note that even if the son of a deceased parent is not yet of Bar Mitzvah age (13) Kaddish Yatom is recited. One of the reasons for this is that the child's prayer can bring a public arousal for the response in the Kaddish of amen. Historically, amen is a critically important statement in Judaism which became so universal that it was incorporated into Christian prayers, which basically means we believe in the truth in praise of God.

The foregoing is historically fascinating since we see that the Kaddish ritual originated progressively in Germany (Ashkenazi) was transferred to Spain (Sephardic) and transferred into a universal halacha. The work of the Rama was crucial in the Ashkenazi acceptance process. Later on we see the same Christian influence taking place with the Jaskur prayer.

When we traced the mystery of Kaddish prayer, we became fascinated by the fact that when a Jewish halachic ritual is applied to Talmudic text to form a new Jewish custom is halachically mandated within a few hundred years. We see how important and vital the Kaddish prayer became that it was a fundamental prayer for both Sephardic and Ashkenazi Jews and remains so to this day.

It became the prayer for every Jew whether he or she be learned or not. This remarkable change became, in the authors' opinion, a historical breakthrough in the practice of Judaism and contributed immensely for the ability for one to personalize and be part of community spirituality in the same process. It was also considered revolutionary since it eradicated any necessary qualifications to recite the prayer, allowing and mandating the opportunity to all.

The *Kaddish* was also recited over the Jews of Magenza who committed suicide and therefore martyred themselves (sometimes killing one another in order not to fall into gentile hands). For example: Meri Yosef and Rabbi Yehuda HaLevi Ben Rabbenu Shmuel, Rav Peter, Rav Efraim from Buna, Rav Yosef HaCohen from France, and others. These events caused a total transformation of the Jewish approach toward memorializing the dead.

In that period, the *Kaddish* or memorial prayers were said by the elite group, mainly the rabbis and the scholars, and the common man had no similar opportunity to express his grief.[70] The Jewish common man observed that the Christian community, both its leaders and its followers, had a method of expressing their grief in a common form. Because of this, the rabbis were compelled to modify their approach to memorial prayers. They had to allow the common man to participate. Otherwise, one could suspect that the Jews might convert to Christianity in order to psychologically participate in the grieving process.

The elasticity and brilliance of the rabbis and what they did at this point was to modify the memorial to allow the common man to participate. One of the main reasons for this was to prevent discrimination and acrimony between the scholars and the men not versed in the Bible. The overwhelming crisis because of the rampant deaths that were taking place amongst the Jews persuaded the rabbis and scholars to open Judaism to the ordinary person and transform the Jewish traditional rituals from the elite to the masses.

This planted the seeds of the Chassidic movements. At first, the prayer was recited at the end of the *shiva* and later at the funeral site and during the *shiva* as well. From this custom grew a version of the *Kaddish* no longer in use called the

"Burial *Kaddish*." Eventually the "Mourner's *Kaddish*" was incorporated into the prayer book and became the cornerstone of Jewish mourning rituals.

This prayer was all the more needed because gentiles and other religious cultures all had a formal prayer ritual for their dead. The Christian formalized a mourning process. In a study of all religion, one discovers that rituals prayers at death and mourning observances are cross cultural.

An irony and paradox in the way *Kaddish* developed is that directly or indirectly the leaders of the Jewish communities observed their Christian neighbors for guidance in responding to the desperation and anguish stirred up by the horrific massive deaths they were encountering.

Thus we see the slow organic growth of the *Kaddish* which before those times was only recited after the study of Talmud. Faced with masses of dead Jews who died by means other than self-sacrifice the question remained as to what to say at the ever-increasing number of funerals. What was there to say when the Holy Books and holy artifacts were plundered, torn, and desecrated and then brought for burial?

Luminary rabbinical figures such as Rabbi Mordechai Ben Shemuel of Fulda, Germany, lamented about the fact that there was no formal ritual to memorialize the dead. In Vaucluse, France, Rabbi Hachoen, a rabbinical leader, started the ritual of saying *Kaddish* after the "blood libel." He is reported to have said "it is strange that we have to adopt '*hukot hagoyiim*'" (laws of gentiles). Two other rabbis, Rabbi Yousef and Rabbi Yehuda Ha'Levi Ben Rabbenu Shmuel replied, "Let's study the habits of non-believers. Observe how they are memorializing their deceased, and let us bring 'kina' or prayer, to express Jewish agony."[71]

Faced with such a dilemma, the rabbis Mordechai ben-

Hillel (from Nuremberg) and Rabbi Shmuel ben-David were asked to look at "*hukot hagoyim*," among the laws of the gentiles. One can see from this instruction from the rabbis that at that period of time, the study of the ways and religious customs of the gentiles, was a legitimate mandate of study. The rabbis sought to find appropriate prayers for the Jewish burial ceremony to replace the customary "*Kinot*" or "*slikhot*."[72]

So we see the need for the Jews to find a prayer that would allow them to express their sorrow over the loss of brethren. It may seem a bit ironic that this truly great prayer of *Kaddish* may have been inspired by the Christians and was appropriately sought from the Christians from the direction of Rabbi Shmuel ben-David. It is believed that he chose the *Kaddish* because it expresses a pure faith in God despite catastrophe, slaughter, and plague.

In addition, after the cruel killings by the oppressor Rindfleisch (1298), Rabbi Moshe ben-Yitzhak declared that although the Christians referred to us as "the devil's children," they did have a prayer to say after their loved ones died that appeared to satisfy the spirit, while the Jews did not. Therefore, Jews should imitate their custom by having a special prayer of their own.

After the killing of hundreds of Jews when the community of Wurzburg was demolished, Rabbenu Asher commanded the saying of the *Kaddish*. It is interesting to note that the Christians began to notice that the Jews were reciting the *Kaddish* following their slaughter and forbid them to say "The Great God." This was in the text of the *Kaddish* at that time, but the Christians said this was an expression attributed to Jesus and, therefore, forbidden to the Jews.

The custom of "mentioning, remembering the souls," the *Yizkor*, four times a year (last day of Passover, Shavuot, Yom

Kippur, and Shmini Atzeret) whereby one prays for the peaceful rest for the deceased's soul as well as for its elevation, was established in Ashkenazi communities after the Crusades.

This started in the 11th century.[73] The names of the fallen at the hands of the crusaders were noted and recorded by congregations and the following was recited: "May God remember the souls of the anonymous and in return his soul will be bound in the Bond of Life." The names were read out between Passover and Atzeret, names of both commoners and dignitaries. Added onto the Sabbath prayers was the "Av Ha'Rachamim" ("Our Merciful Father") prayer, inserted after the Tatnu (the counting in the Hebrew calendar 4856) decrees in Germany (1396).

The *Kaddish* was important because it challenged evil fortune defiantly by praising God in the face of disaster. If it was what God chose, it was ultimately good. In time, the *Kaddish* was said over a span of twelve months. This was a psychological process for grief to take place after which would follow comfort and deference to the face of God.

"The memory of the dead does not depart from the heart until after twelve months" (*Berachot*) and the *Gemara* adds "during the twelve months, the body [of the deceased] exists and his soul rises and falls" (*Shabbat*).

As years passed, the period of reciting the *Kaddish* during the first year was reduced to a period of eleven months. Why? In order to prevent slander against the parents, as though they were wicked, for it is written: "The trial of the wicked in Hell is twelve months" (*Aduyot*). By halting the *Kaddish* after eleven months, one is essentially saying that those who died while sanctifying God's name were acquitted at trial and were no longer in Hell.

How indeed could they be sentenced to Hell when they had sacrificed their lives in the name of God? The Ari, at a later time, ruled that the "*Yartzheit*," the *Kaddish* recited on the anniversary of the death, elevates the deceased to a higher rung in Heaven. As it is written, "a son exonerates his father" and allows him to inherit life in the world to come.

So the motif of comfort became more and more prevalent so that people could be relieved from despair with this outlet for their grief. Now, as then, "may His great Name grow exalted and sanctified"—the King of Kings will bring salvation. The grief over the dead before us shall pass and from the crisis and mourning we will return to hope and return to the course of normal life. To symbolize this cycle it is customary to eat things, such as an egg, during the *shiva*.

So the message is "Do not despair!" The Kingdom of God is spread throughout the world and will achieve the rotation and stability of life as it is written: "May He give reign to His kingship in your lifetimes and in your days."

No angry finger pointing toward the Heavens but rather pacification—a feeling of peace. Therefore the *Kaddish* is only recited in public, with a congregation of at least ten adult males.[74] Thus is formed a shared fate, a bond, an identification with those, like us, whose world was lost. They, like us, must accept the reality that death will always arrive. It will always be with us. Should it arrive before its due time or take an innocent life, then by saying the *Kaddish* we will raise the image of the dead and dispatch him or her on a journey that is spiritual, rhythmic, and cyclical.

"God has given and God has taken away—may the Name of the Lord be blessed forever and ever." It is necessary to accept what happens even when the damage seems irreversible and especially difficult. This is what is referred to as the "justification of judgment," where we declare that God knows the soul and its inner workings, rewards and punishments, the laws of recompense. If God therefore rules that a life should end, we must accept this "forever and ever." "In the world that He created as He willed." A world created with laws even if we do not understand the logic or purpose behind them.

The *Kaddish* is a catharsis that cleanses and purifies—an accepted element of the Jewish experience. The world, it seems, cannot exist without agony, and suffering is a hand-maiden of life. Death, wickedness, darkness form a striking contrast to the daily routine, the banal, the pleasurable, and hedonistic. Death is an event requiring mental coping—it removes the "rust" encrusted onto our thought processes.

Women were allowed to recite the *Kaddish* when the deceased left behind no sons, and this is practical and brings peace to the soul. There were lawmakers who insisted that women could gather a *minyan* only in their homes and recite the *Kaddish* but only outside of a synagogue, a public space reserved for men. But women were no less victims of both the Crusades and the Black Plague and it seemed quite natural that they too should be permitted by custom to recite the *Kaddish*.

Sages spoke of the impurity of the dead only in physiological terms. Many asked the following: If a Jew lived a pure life, free of sin, why then did he or she have to pay with his or her lifes?[75]

One must understand that this purity is found only in the soul which resides in the physical body—the body is merely a vessel. When a person departs from this world, the soul rises above while the body remains frozen in rigidity. It is because the soul no longer resides within it that the body is transformed into an impure thing, even if death occurred while he victim was sanctifying God. The elimination of death in the future is one of the signs of the Redemption as is written in the "Vision of the Dry Bones" (Ezekiel).

During the Crusades, the *Kaddish* was appropriate during the period of burial and the sitting of *shiva* because it symbolized continuity. A son exonerates his father and so the dynasty continues. The sins of the fathers remain but the freedom to choose and act is in the hands of the sons, the freedom to amend and to follow in the path of the just. A son's *Kaddish* helps atone for the sins of his father and therefore it is "the privilege of the sons." "As long as one's seed is alive, so too is one alive."

Whoever leaves his spiritual inheritance in the hands of his sons is not dead. Rather, he has a continuity that gives meaning to his former life and actions. The concept of continuity was especially important during the Crusades, when whole families were wiped out. The *Kaddish* expresses the valuable and good in the father's life while at the same time begging forgiveness for his sins.

This applies not only to the mourner, who in essence includes the entire congregation by having them answer Amen to the praising of God. "Blessed, praised, glorified, exalted, extolled, mighty, upraised, and lauded be the Name of the Holy One, Blessed is He." Therefore the sanctification of God becomes public, general, a shared statement of friends who share a common faith. The *Kaddish* served to unify the congregation during tumultuous times, unifying parents and children, unifying one congregation member with another.

There is a strong educational element at work here. The agony, the deliberations, the doubts, all these are bound to lead to a greater truth—the darkness will rise from the depths and transform into a great light. Death is a symptom of evil and suffering one must leap, however, from the depths of the netherworld to the zenith of the Heavens.

"On my one foot I stand in seventh heaven while on the other, in the netherworld." So says the Admor from Kotzk. So will the bereaved arrive at the true knowledge of the God who has taken from him a loved one—the bereaved will come to an understanding of true faith, of God's justice, and of theological puzzles such as "concealment of the face"—God's face, that is.

A prime example of that is the Holocaust. There are those who claim that God hid from the suffering of his children during that catastrophe. "*Tziduk Ha'Din*" ("Justification of justice") is another riddle to some. It appears at times that God punishes good and rewards evil. The answer to them is one: Evil and death are necessary but the *Kaddish* reminds us that death is not necessarily a punishment but rather a natural, normal course of events.[76]

"And it is a good thing—such is death" (*Beresheit Raba*). The deaths that occurred during the crusades and Black Plague were part of the cycle of life; they were by no means punishment. "It is better to visit a house of mourning than it is to visit a house of drinking and merriment" because the living can learn a lesson from the dead.

We have just described some of the events of the Crusades and Black Plague[77] in order to give a brush stroke of the times when the *Kaddish* was adopted as a prayerful response to death. It is important to note that the prayer is not meant to address the dead for it is forbidden under Jewish law to conjure, to worship those no longer living. Here the just, the dead, is but a tool and agent in order to reach up to God in his Heaven.

· 16 ·

More on the Crusades and Kaddish

*A*NOTHER CONNECTION OF the *Kaddish* prayer is a link to the Crusades with "*Aseret Harugey Malchut*" (the Ten *Tana'im* [Jewish Scholars] who were executed during the period of Hadrian, the Roman Caesar, after the failure of Bar-Kohva's rebellion). One can find these *piutim* in the Yom Kippur Prayer Book. Special liturgical hymns—*piutim*— were written for this occasion acknowledging the rightness of the Divine Judgment (*Tsiduk Ha'Din*), i.e. the Destruction of the Second Mikdash, by Rabbi Se'adya Ga'on.

The purpose of these *piutim* was to remove any criticism of the Divine Judgment. Incidentally, the killing of *Aseret Harugey Malchut* is referred to the Biblical occurrence of the sale of Yoseph by his ten brothers for which they were never punished.

The recital of the *Kaddish* during the Crusades and the Black Plague links also with the midrashic source on Rabbi Akiva: "[It is told that] Rabbi Akiva salvaged a dead man from Hell by having the dead man's son face the public and tell them to Bless God and they repeated after him: Blessed be God the Blessed (*The Vitri Makhzor*, p. 113)." This Midrash of Rabbi Akiva and the dead man is only one example of a son's ability to commend his dead father and by that relieve him from his heavy punishment.

A connection of the midrashic story or the *Kaddish* and the Crusades was made because in those days, many children became orphans after their parents were killed, and it was accepted that charity for the dead, mentioning them in prayer and the recital of *Kaddish*, *Yizkor*, and *Av Harachamim* all contribute to the acquittal of the parents in the Divine Judgment.[78]

"Katan" [a minor child] saves his father from his retributions (*Machzor Vitri*). From this derived the Ashkenazi custom that on Saturday night an orphan (of both parents) child leads the prayer in the synagogue to recite the *Kaddish* so as to help his parents at this "time of will" on Saturday night when the dead go back to their places after the Sabbath.

As mentioned earlier, the *Kaddish* contains also the acknowledgement of the rightness of the Divine Judgment. In *Tehilim* (Psalms) 38: "Misfortune and grief I will find and the name of God I shall call," and Job (39) said: "God has given and God has taken. Be the name of God Blessed."

This is the reason why it is said at the home of the mourners "*Baruch Dayan Emet*" (Blessed be the True Judge) and "*Baruch Hatov ve-Hametiv*" (Blessed be the Good and the Good Doer). In addition, the mourner acknowledges the rightness of the judgment by saying "*Yitgadal ve-Yitkadash Shmey Raba*." And

Rav Amram Ga'on writes: When the burial of the dead is finished, the *Sheliach Zibur* (The public messenger) says "*Yitgadal*" (*Kaddish*) after the prayer "*Ziduk Hadin*." This *Kaddish* is similar to *Kaddish deRabanan*" ("*Be-alma de-Atid lehadeta*") and it connects with the times of the Crusades when people needed all their spiritual as well as physical strength.

The *Kaddish* prayer filled their needs. In it there is the "*Ziduk Hadin*" in the words "*Yitgadal ve-itkadash Shmei Raba*" which came from the book of the Prophet Yehezkiel (38, 23): "*ve'itgadalti ve'itkadashti*" (I shall be turning greater and holier).

When the farmers said after the first rains came down: *Yitgadal ve'itkadash ve'itromem Shimcha Malchenu*, they added another verse of this prayer from the Talmud *Yerushalmi*, Masechet Sota: "*Baruch Shem Kvod Malchenu Le'olam Va'ed*" to the Aramaic version: "*Ye'he Shem Raba Mevorach le'Olam v'Olamim*".

We found another place, in the book of *Daniel Beyt*, 20: on the exile of Bavel (Babylon) when he said in Aramaic is praise of the Almighty: "*Leheve shme di-Eloho Mevorach min Alma Ve'ad Alma*." All these quotations which strengthened from call to response, that give glory to God, and was recited, according to Masechet Sofrim, after learning the Torah or reading it in the synagogues. Rav Nathan Habavli said that when the *Reish Galuta* (Head of the Exile) ended their speech, they too said *Kaddish*. From this derived the ritual of saying *Kaddish* at the beginning of every journey of the Crusades in the hope that it would stop the riots [pogroms] that accompanied them.

The *Kaddish* started off as a prayer for an important Jewish victim but gradually became a fixed prayer for all victims.

· 17 ·

THE JEW AS A NON-CITIZEN AND THE CHURCH SYNOD

*T*HE FIRST PART of our search for answers about the *Kaddish* had taken us from Israel to Europe and Turkey. We had come away with a deeper understanding of our subject in the context of traditional practices of Judaism and related material in the literature of Judaism—the Bible, the Talmud, midrashic sources, and folk tales. But there remained a major gap to be filled—the historical background.

During the Middle Ages and through the 15th and 16th centuries, one tragic event after another became a story of persecuted Jews. And it became clear that from this suffering grew the need for a core statement of unswerving faith. From books, interviews, and the examination of centuries-old texts, the answers emerge.

While historians argue about whether it is appropriate to refer to the Middle Ages as the "Dark Ages," there is no doubt that the latter designation is entirely appropriate in terms of the Jews of Christian Europe during that time. Buffeted on all sides, caught between massive forces, subject to the whims of despotic rulers and churchmen, accused of heinous crimes and often convicted despite the facts, Jews were banished whenever it suited the local ruler, as a way to seize assets or to assuage tension within his territory. They were often forced to wear clothing which singled them out and to live in severely restricted areas in the shabbiest sections of towns and cities, open to massacre at the instigation of rabble-rousers.

These centuries were bitter ones for Jews. To better understand the historical reasons for the development of the Kaddish, especially the "Mourner's" *Kaddish* during that time, it is essential that we examine the life of the Jews in that era and the milieu and the society in which they found themselves.

Though there was little concept of democracy or of citizenship in the Middle Ages, local residents in some areas did retain rights and privileges. Jews were not given that chance. Rather, they were regarded in one of two ways: either as an alien presence, one which might undermine the authority of the church, and as such had to be repressed; or alternately, as members of another nation, i.e., literally as aliens allowed to live among their non-Jewish neighbors under forbearance.[79]

In the former case, where Jews were seen as a "corrupting" force, one which might shake the faith of their neighbors, the authorities felt it their religious duty to deny civil rights to Jews. These civil rights were few for non-Jewish peasants but almost non-existent for Jews.

Jews were considered foreign creatures. They were limited in what they were allowed to do to earn a living. They were limited in where they could live. They were limited in when and where they could travel. All their so-called rights were granted by the local or national ruler—and could be cancelled at a hiccup. Even owning things was tenuous, for the property of Jews could be seized by the authorities for any reason or no reason at all.

In place after place, the head man would say to the Jews, sometimes on just a passing impulse: "You can't live here." Hitler refined it to, "You can't live."

One of the side effects of the Holocaust was the seizure of Jewish property. It was Rudi Vrba, the first man ever to escape from Auschwitz, who pointed out that when a Jewish family was arrested and shipped to a death camp, the Nazis seized the family possessions. They would confiscate a toaster to reward this Nazi follower and a typewriter to reward that one. This was not a small thing, Vrba points out, for the era was one of severe shortages, since all manufacturing was geared to support the war effort. The Jews had almost no rights at all in the Middles Ages and fewer such rights in Hitler's Germany.

But two hundred years ago, the very survival of Jewry was a miracle. Restrictions against Jews were varied but existed in Germany, England, Austria, Spain, Portugal, Italy, and France during the Middle Ages.

Restrictions against Jews had their beginnings long ago. They existed even in Greek cities early during the Christian era. Never mind that Jesus was a Jew. Jews were often not permitted to practice their religious customs. Even living space for Jews was severely restricted. Occasionally, a generous king or kindly ruler would grant a few rights and privileges to the Jewish population, but these were never equal to those given to their Greek neighbors.

During the reign of the Roman Emperor Caracalla (211–217 C.E.), the Jews, for the first time, were granted the right to become full Roman citizens. Emperor Hadrian, however, fearful that too many Romans might be attracted to Judaism, put an end to this by forbidding circumcision. Jews would not submit to this decree, and ultimately the law was amended to forbid only the circumcision of non-Jews.[80]

Special taxes were imposed on Jews throughout the Roman Empire, but these were supposedly earmarked for the development of what was then known as Palestine. Soon, though, these taxes were appropriated by the empire for its own uses.

Whatever rights the Jews accrued during this early period were quickly whittled away when the Emperor Constantine made Christianity the official religion of Rome. Legislation was introduced which favored Christians and discriminated against Jews. For example, in 404 C.E. the law was amended to forbid Jews from holding public office, since it was now considered wrong for a Jew to give orders to a Christian. Jews were forbidden to attempt to convert Christians, to marry Christians, to keep slaves, or even to build synagogues.

As an added incentive for Jews to convert to Christianity, their parents were not permitted to disinherit the converts, even if they wanted to do so. Jews were not permitted to testify against Christians, and a special oath, calling down upon the individual all types of curses should he lie, was instituted just for Jews. The Jews who converted in Spain, who are referred to as *conversos*, and the Jews in Turkey who converted to Islam, referred to as the *donma*, kept the *Kaddish*,

Yom Kippur, and Passover, underground, notwithstanding their forced conversion and at great risk. Thus we see *Kaddish* was elevated to the highest form of ritual and was kept as part of the religious historical unity.

· 18 ·

The Church Synods

THROUGHOUT THE CENTURIES, beginning with the Apostles' Synods, mentioned in the New Testament, church synods, councils of church officials, have attempted to write canon law for the church. Many of these synods dealt with the Jews, and over the centuries their regulations became ever more hostile and onerous.

At the beginning of the 4th century C.E., a synod at Elvira, for example, forbade all daily contact with Jews, such as Christians and Jews eating at the same table. By the time of the fourth synod in Toledo, in 633, it was decreed that even though Jews were not to be forcibly converted, anyone who had been baptized—forcibly or not—must remain a Christian.

Anyone who protected Jews would be excommunicated. The last synod in Toledo, before Spain was conquered by the Moors, was held in 681. It attempted to destroy all vestiges of Judaism. Thus, it forbade anyone from observing the Jewish Sabbath or Jewish festivals, or observing Jewish dietary laws, or working on Sunday. Furthermore, it forbade any Jew from emigrating.[81]

Four hundred years later, the third Lateran Council, in 1179, again forbade Jews to have Christians as servants, excommunicated any Christian living among Jews, and gave credence to the testimony of a Christian over that of a Jew.

Since Christian princes claimed the right to the property of all Jews who had converted to Christianity, this was counterproductive when the church sought more converts. The Council then declared that the property of a convert should remain his.

One ruling of that Council in a way actually helped the Jews. It decreed that any Christian lending money at interest would not be given a Christian burial. This, of course, was an immense help to Jewish moneylenders, and moneylending was one of the limited number of professions allowed Jews in many countries.

All of this laid the groundwork for the fourth Lateran Council of 1215, which, in essence, removed the Jew from the realm of humanity. It was a precursor to the Nazi laws against the Jews. First, the Jews had to wear a special hat and badge, which were designed to single them out as objects of ridicule.

The Council claimed that Jews made a point of parading in their best finery on Christian holidays, so the Jews were confined to their ghetto homes throughout those days. That synod, in the interest of helping the Crusaders, forced Jews to forgo all interest on loans made to Christians, thus making it easier to finance the Crusaders on their mission.

In 1267, about half a century later, the Council of Vienna extended these rules even further. It forbade Jews from staying at Christian inns or baths, and ordered Jews to remain home with their doors and windows closed when the Host was carried outside. Furthermore, by a decree of a synod in 1276, Jews were allowed to live only in large towns because by living in villages they might lead the simple folk astray.

Later synods forbade Jews from living near churches or graveyards, and even later ones decreed that they should live in separate areas—the forerunners of the ghetto. Other synods of that era forbade Jews to eat meat—or even to carry it across the street—on Christian fast days. A later synod forbade Jews to sell meat.

Soon public pressure led to active demands that all Jews be converted. The General Council in Basel in 1434 adopted a requirement for the Jews to attend compulsory sermons aimed at having them convert.[82]

The synod in Milan in 1565 served both to reiterate the prohibitions of previous synods (especially as many of the rules had been ignored) and added new prohibitions. Thus it was again decreed that no Jew could employ a Christian servant, and that no Christians might live among the Jews. It was also ruled that no new synagogues could be built, old ones could only be repaired when they were totally dilapidated, and that under no condition could they be beautified.

This synod was "kind enough" to specify that Jews should be physically protected, but only "out of common humanity."

Historically, the pattern became crystal clear. Church edicts throughout the centuries were designed to add to previous strictures, making living conditions for the Jews more miserable and more precarious.

· 19 ·

THE CRUSADES—SUFFERING CREATES PRAYER

$\mathcal{W}$HILE HISTORY BOOKS sometimes view the Crusades as a romantic—if not to say somewhat quixotic—quest to free the Holy Land, complete with heroes such as Richard the Lion-hearted, those episodes were an unmitigated calamity to Jewish populations.

Christian Crusaders were bent on freeing the Holy Land of "infidels," but on their way they sought to "cleanse" their lands of Jews by massacring them wherever they were found. Goaded by religious fanatics, the mobs that made up the Crusaders dealt death to all Jews in their paths.

The Jews of Germany, France, and England suffered the most. Not only were thousands killed, but the hatred engendered among the Crusaders against the Jews became a staple in the relationships between Christians and Jews in the centuries that followed. By the same token, Jews were left with nothing but fear and hatred of Christians.

In this way, the Crusades marked the major turning point in the way the two religions related to one another. In France, Peter the Hermit, along with Pope Urban II, issued a call at the Council of Clermont in 1094 to free the Holy Land. Godfrey de Bouillion then declared that he would indeed avenge the blood of Jesus, by not leaving a single Jew alive. His colleagues swore to have the Jews either convert or be killed. Those who joined this campaign all affixed a cross to their clothing, and thus originated the name "Crusaders."

The Jews, a small minority in a sea of Christians, could do little to prevent these attacks. Even so, in January 1096, Jews declared a fast day, and tried to bribe de Bouillion into abandoning his plans. When he arrived in their cities, the Jewish communities of Cologne and Mayence (Mainz) each gave him a gift of 500 silver florins. It was an enormous sum of money at the time.

Early in the spring of 1096, however, the rabble making up the First Crusade finally struck. They killed 22 Jews in Metz. Then, on May 3, they struck at the Jews of Speyer, and killed 11. It was only through the intervention of Bishop John that the rest of the Jews were spared.

On May 18, the Crusaders attacked the Jews of Worms. A number were killed. A few were forcibly converted while others committed suicide rather than submit to forced conversion. Some Jews managed to take refuge in the castle of the local bishop, but the castle was stormed a week later and all its occupants were killed. The list of names of those killed numbered 400, but it was believed that twice that number were actually murdered.

Of course, the property of all the dead Jews was seized and their houses burned down. One family was literally roasted alive, while the rabble jeered and kept exhorting them to convert if they wanted to escape their flaming deaths. That same day, May 18, a group of Crusaders arrived at the outskirts of Mayence. Archbishop Ruthard had promised to protect the Jews, and refused to allow the Crusaders entry. Two days later the Crusaders forced open a side gate.

Even though the Jews resisted, all but 54 who had managed to hide in the cathedral treasure house were killed. Some of the Jews who had been fighting the angry mob for an entire day committed suicide when they knew they were over-whelmed. The number of Jews killed is said to have been over a thousand. One of them, who had been forcibly baptized, burned down his home and the synagogue and perished in the flames rather than allow the synagogue to be converted into a church.[83]

The Second Crusade, about half a century after the First (1145–1147) was not as disastrous for the Jews. While a monk named Rudolph went about the Rhine Valley preaching that Jews should be killed as enemies of the Christian religion, Bernard of Clairvaux actively argued against this, saying it was unchristian behavior. In the end, only a relatively small number of Jewish communities suffered. For example, the Jews of Magdeburg and Halle were expelled from their cities. In spite of Bernard's efforts, when the Crusaders came to Wurtzburg they killed 22 Jews there, including the town's rabbi and his wife and children.

It was due to the intervention of Emperor Frederick I, who had received a very sizable sum of money from the Jews, that all were offered protection—and this message was passed on by all the bishops. Indeed, Frederick stated that any Christian who killed a Jew would be put to death. During this Crusade, the famous Tosafist, Rabbenu Tam, the grandson of Rashi, was nearly killed. He was saved by a friendly knight's intervention. Nevertheless, he received five stab wounds in memory of the way Jesus had been stabbed.

Pope Innocent III was quite willing to help the Crusaders at the expense of the Jews. He ordered that all loans made by Jews to Crusaders were to be interest-free, and that any interest paid until the time of his edict was to be refunded. This meant that the Jews would get their principal back but only later after years of waiting and without interest. By contrast, the Jews of England were left undisturbed by this Crusade.

In addition to the physical harm done to the Jewish populations during the Crusades, and the economic deprivations that followed, the institution of the "ghetto" became formalized. It translated into a severe limitation of Jewish living space.

· 20 ·

The Ghetto

$\mathcal{P}$RIOR TO THE Crusades, the Jews had enjoyed a rich harvest of trade. However when the Crusaders reached Palestine, they too became major traders. This seriously hampered business in that area. The Crusades, then, affected the Jews on many levels including economically.

As we noted above, in the Germanic lands, the Jews had no rights whatsoever, unless they had bought each specific right. Such rights might be given to an individual Jew, to a group of Jews, or to all the Jews of a district. However, except for these rights, the Jews were not entitled to any protection under the law.

The name "ghetto"[84] might be derived from the area in which the Jews in Venice were forced to live in the late 11th century. The word itself may refer to a nearby cannon foundry (*ghetto* or *getto*) or even be derived from the Hebrew *get*—a divorce document—as this practice "divorced" the Jews from the other residents of the city.

The ghetto was usually located in the worst district of each city. By plan, it was very crowded. The area was deliberately carved out to provide much less space than the needs of its population.

In Rome, for example, the ghetto was located in a neighborhood that was flooded every year by the Tiber. In many instances, the ghetto was surrounded by a wall of some type, with gates locked each night. By local law, ghetto dwellers thus had to be inside the gates each night.

On the one hand this limited the Jews' mobility, but on the other the wall and gates did serve as some protection against attack. The crowded conditions in the ghetto, with narrow streets and houses built in very close proximity to one another, were the cause of numerous fires which devastated entire communities, including those in Frankfurt, Nikolsburg, and Prague (twice).[85]

As to the purpose of the ghetto, a very interesting 1570 document (written in Vienna) describes the discussion that took place about locating the ghetto outside the city. There were three objections to this idea. They offer insight into what motivated the makers of the ghetto. The three objections were: a) outside the city, the Jews might more readily engage in "nefarious practices"; b) the Jews might be surprised by their enemies; and c), the Jews might escape! The latter is the most interesting!

Strange as it may seem to us today, from time to time the Jews themselves wanted a ghetto established. Living "outside," with gentiles, meant being insulted daily, sometimes being falsely accused of crimes, and indeed being open to physical abuse against which there was generally no recourse within the legal system.

Of course, having all the Jews in one place made it easier for the authorities to carry out an expulsion, as happened in Vienna in 1625 and in Prague in 1744.

With the Emancipation in the 19th century, the ghetto as an institution came to an end, until the Nazis revived it with lethal force during World War II.[86]

· 21 ·

BLOOD LIBEL AND THE MASSACRE OF JEWS

*A*s IF ALL of the disabilities and limitations to which the Jews were subject during the Middle Ages and after were not enough, they were particular victims of all types of false accusations. And these could result in penalties ranging from fines to confiscation of property to expulsion and even to death and massacre.

One of the most potent of anti-Semitic slanders concerned Christian attitudes toward communion. In Catholic belief, the communion wine and wafer (the "Host") used at the Mass are mysteriously transubstantiated into the blood and flesh of Jesus. Not surprisingly, these two items inspired a deeply spiritual emotion among all Christians. Playing on the sanctity of these two elements of Catholic ritual, unscrupulous individuals spread rumors that the Jews in a particular community, in a deliberate act of defilement, had taken the Host and had "stabbed" it. Folklore states that it actually "bled."

While to the modern eye this charge may seem ludicrous, in the Middle Ages such accusations resulted in the deaths of thousands of Jews. It did not require much to create a case against the Jews. All that one had to do was to plant a piece of the Host on some unsuspecting Jew and to then "find" it on him or in his home—especially when one knew exactly where to look.[87]

So intent were the authorities to convict the Jews, and so harshly had they been portrayed by the church leaders, that the source of the accusation was irrelevant: a thief, a prostitute, a recent convert to Christianity who wished to show his *bona fides,* someone with a grudge against the Jews, or who owed a sum of money to a Jew—all of these were accepted as having given credible evidence.

Even when the evidence clearly proved the Jew's innocence, it was often disregarded. Furthermore, where no evidence was available, the accused would be tortured until he "confessed." Once a conviction had been obtained, it served as an open invitation to attack all nearby Jews and to plunder their earthly goods. At the very least, the "guilty" Jew would be burned at the stake, and in many cases the same fate met all his co-religionists.

In 1215 Pope Innocent III declared the doctrine of transubstantiation, and as a result of that doctrine the peasants and others began to make the Host an object of public worship—the "very flesh and blood" of Jesus. It did not take long for this doctrine and its implications to seep into Christian consciousness, and with it, the opportunity to harm the Jews. The first documented case of an accusation against Jews happened in 1243. This was 28 years after the doctrine was expounded.

The drama took place in a village called Belitz, near Berlin. As a result, all the Jews of Belitz were burned to death. Other such charges (and the "punishments" which followed) took place, among many others, in Paris in 1290, in Laa, Austria, in 1294, in Cracow in 1330, in Prague in 1399.

Now, lest we think that all of this relates only to the church of the 1200's, 1300's, and 1400's, the fact is that for hundreds of years after that, there were Catholic festivals in commemoration of the "deliverance" from the "desecration of the Host." Indeed, in 1820, such a celebration, lasting eight days, was held in Brabant to commemorate such an event of 1370—or 450 years earlier.

Fifty years later, in 1870, as plans were afoot to mark the five hundredth anniversary of that event. It was conclusively proven that while three Jews had indeed been burned to death in 1370, the charge had nothing to do with the desecration of the Host, and that the original documents had been tampered with to make it appear that that had been the reason for the Jews having been burned. Given clear evidence of forgery, Pope Pius IX halted the festival.

We may add parenthetically that Pius IX (1792–1878) was in many ways helpful to the Jews. It was he who abolished the requirement for Jews to live in ghettos and removed the restrictions against their entering certain professions. He also terminated the law requiring Jews to listen to a conversion sermon four times a year.

It was not all unimpeachable sincerity, however, for he didn't revoke the tax Jews had to pay, which was used to run a school for converts from Judaism. Nor did he revoke the law that said any evidence given by a Jew against a Catholic was inadmissible.

As noted earlier, according to the New Testament, at the time of Jesus' trial and crucifixion, the Jews had exclaimed, "His blood be upon us and our children." The belief in the Middle Ages, obtained from one who was described as "a very learned Jew" who had converted to Christianity—history does not record his name—was that as a result of this utterance, the Jews had been cursed and that Jewish males, like Jewish females, bled each month.

The prevalent belief was that Jews needed the blood of a Christian to stop this hemorrhaging. While we do not know the name of the so-called "learned Jew" who had converted, it is possible that this was Nicholas Donin of La Rochelle, who in 1240 had been involved in a disputation with R. Yehiel of Paris, as a result of which all the extant Talmudic manuscripts in Paris were burned, including many which could never be replaced.

For a time, blood libel trials came fast and furious. One of the more important was that of Little St. Hugh of Lincoln (another "victim of the Jews" who was canonized). Hugh, then eight years old, disappeared in Lincoln on July 31, 1255. His body was found on August 29—almost a month later—in the field of a Jew named Jopin. Needless to say, the body was in an advanced state of decay, and it was not possible to ascertain very much about how or when the child had died.

A judge who happened to be present when the filth-encrusted body was found, John of Lexington, offered Jopin a way of escaping punishment, even though it was his field in which the body had been found. In return for his confession that a gathering of Jews had crucified the boy, John offered Jopin his life. Five weeks later, though, when King Henry III reached Lincoln, he refused to accept the agreement made by the judge and ordered Jopin's execution. Further, 91 Jews of the town were seized and sent to London, where 18 of them were executed. Eventually, the others were pardoned.

Another case in the "blood libel"[88] history occurred less than a century ago, in 1911 in Russia. There, a man named Mendl Beilis was accused of killing a 12-year-old Russian boy on the outskirts of Kiev. Even though the police had clear evidence that the murder had been committed by a gang of thieves, the anti-Semitic minister of justice, Shcheglovitov, had the police channel their investigation into a blood libel charge. When the case came to trial, the prosecuting attorney made a point of trying to prove that the gang involved had not committed the crime.

A Catholic priest with a criminal record testified as to the "truth" of the Jewish "custom." The chief rabbi of Moscow was called to testify, and demolished the priest's testimony, showing that the latter had absolutely no knowledge of the Talmudic texts that he claimed to have quoted. The jury, made up of Russian peasants, took but a short time to declare Beilis not guilty.

Beilis, in spite of his acquittal, felt himself unsafe in Russia. He emigrated to the United States in 1920, where he died in 1934. Incidentally, the fact that Beilis was totally exonerated did not stop the reactionary Russian government under

Nicholas II from continuing to spread those libel among the masses. Only the 1917 revolution that ended the rules of the Czars brought this to a finish. .

And yet, in spite of centuries of evidence against the blood libel charge, it remains a potent tool in the hands of fervent anti-semites in many parts of the world. As an historical aside, it is to be noted that while Jewish law prefers red wine for use during the Passover *seder*, certain medieval rabbis specifically suggested that a white wine replace it, so that the enemies of the Jews should not have any cause for claiming that the Jews had adulterated their wine with blood.[89]

· 22 ·

BLACK DEATH &
JEWISH "CONFESSION"

*T*HE SO-CALLED "Black Death" (the bubonic, septicemia, and pneumonic plagues, all caused by the same bacillus) was a violent pestilence that ravaged Europe between March 1348 and the spring of 1351, and is said to have killed nearly half the population.

The disease was carried by sailors to Genoa from south Russia, having originated in central Asia. During March and April, 1348, it spread through Italy, Spain, and southern France and by May of that year, reached England. Although the Jews might have suffered as much as the non-Jews, the rumor spread that the Black Death was the result of the fact that Jews had "poisoned the wells" in order to kill Christians. Actually, the first suspects had been those who suffered from leprosy, but then the eternal scapegoat, the Jew, became the object of the charge.[90]

A theory has been advanced, incidentally, that the Jews, indeed, did not suffer as much from the Black Death, and for a simple reason—i.e., the extensive, religiously oriented rules about washing and bathing. These included washing one's hands upon arising, after passing water or excrement, and before eating bread. Added to that was the requirement of women to immerse themselves in a *mikveh*, or ritual bath, each month, which, in turn, was preceded by a thorough cleansing of the body. Further, from time immemorial Jews have set aside Friday as a day to bathe in preparation for the Sabbath. There was at least some chance that these practices would diminish the chances of infection.

In the case of the Black Death, a familiar pattern was followed. In 1348, soon after the plague began, various town officials accused the Jews of poisoning the wells, and they were able to "prove" their allegations by a simple means: by torturing Jews until they admitted their "guilt."

When the plague reached Pillon, a number of Jews were arrested and tortured into "confessing." A person named Balavignus broke under torture and claimed that the dreadful plague was the result of a plot by three Jews to poison the water supply all over Europe. According to him, the "recipe" they had used consisted of Christians' hearts, spiders, frogs, lizards, human flesh, and sacred Hosts. These, he claimed, had been made into a powder, which had been used to poison the wells from which Christians drew their water. In Zurich, this charge was coupled with the blood libel, and a number of

Jews were burned there on September 21, 1348. Those not burned were expelled from the city.

These "confessions" were sent from town to town, and within a month there were massacres of Jews in no fewer than 80 cities and towns. On January 22, 1349, the Jews of Speyer, Germany, were given the choice of baptism or death. Many chose death, while others committed suicide rather than convert. A few did, indeed, agree to baptism. In Freiberg, all the Jews, except 12 of the richest, were killed on January 30, 1349. The 12 were not saved because of their wealth, but only so that the extent of their wealth could be ascertained and then confiscated.

Of course, once some Jews had "confessed," the news spread like wildfire, convincing most non-Jews that the cause of the plague had been found. In Strasburg, the local mayor refused to believe these reports and was deposed.

In the depredation that followed, on February 16, 1349, 2,000 Jews were slaughtered. As an indication of the true motivation underlying such an action, all promissory deeds held by Jews against local Christians were destroyed, thus canceling all the debts. Furthermore, to ensure that the massacre went on unhindered, those who owed the Jews money assured those who would take part that they would not be prosecuted.

The city of Worms was next, and 400 Jews were killed there on March 1, 1349. In July, when the mob turned on the Jews in Frankfurt, the potential victims organized to defend themselves, rather than stand by passively. While many Jews were killed, they did manage to strike out at their enemies and to burn down a good part of the city.

The largest slaughter took place in Mayence (Meinz),

where, on August 22, 1349, no fewer than 6,000 Jews died. Here, though, the Jews did not only lash out at the non-Jews' property, but actively fought their tormentors, resulting in the deaths of 200 of the attackers. Finally, when the Jews felt that they were unable to break out of the cordon enveloping the ghetto, with the only other alternatives being starvation or baptism, they set fire to their homes and perished in the flames. Later, the Jews of Cologne were massacred, as were 3,000 Jews in Erfurt. Finally, after mass killings of Jews in Nuremberg, Hanover, and Brussels, the mob fury receded and the massacres came to an end.

· 23 ·

THE EXPULSION FROM SPAIN

*F*ROM THE MIDDLE Ages on, until as recently as the 1840s, it was not uncommon for all Jews to be expelled from towns and cities, and sometimes even from entire countries. At least 25 such expulsions are recorded, from areas in Russia, France, Germany, and even Switzerland. These took place from the 1100s on and ended only 160 years ago. The motivation for such action was both religious and economic, with the Jews as natural scapegoats.

By far the most important of the expulsions was that from Spain. This took place in 1492, and brought with it dramatic changes in the history of the Jewish people, as well as in the culture and political life of Spain and the entire Mediterranean region.[91]

The events of 1492 had roots in the Inquisition, one of the more shameful phases of European Catholic history. When originally constituted, the Vatican's Office of the Inquisition, was not at all aimed at Jews. At that time, it had a mandate to uproot heresy, especially in the ranks of the Albigenses in southern France. Rather, the Inquisitors were engaged almost exclusively in investigating Christians, with a few side forays to burn Jewish works if they were deemed to be anti-Christian. In fact Canon Law specifically forbade the Inquisitors to deal with the Jews.

As the heavy hand of the Inquisition exhausted its victims among the Christian population, the Inquisition needed a new focus. At first it turned its eye on those Jews who had converted to Christianity and showed symptoms of regressing to their former religion, as well as to those Jews who were rumored to be attempting to persuade non-Jews to convert to Judaism.

There were few of such Jews but there were indeed a goodly number who had become Christian by force, and who might indeed practice Jewish rituals in secret. These were the so-called *Marranos*. In 1276, a number of such "backsliding Christians" were burned at the stake, and in 1288 thirteen Jewish "heretics" were burned in Troyes. And in 1310, a converted Jew who had returned to the faith of his fathers was burned at the stake.

Soon the Canon Law restricting the Inquisition from dealing with Jews was conveniently overlooked. It was decided that the Jews, by their very existence, posed a danger to the belief system of pious Christians. Thus, the Inquisition was able to seek out Jews as well as Christian heretics.

A New Inquisition in the recently united provinces of Castile, Aragon, and Navarre was introduced by King Ferdinand V. This Inquisition set its sights on the thousands of Jews who were converts to Christianity and had converted only to save their lives. Most of these so-called "conversos" or "Marranos" (a name of derision) or "New Christians" still held themselves to be Jews and secretly observed Jewish rituals.

Some had advanced to important levels in the king's court, often through alliances with nobles. But their wealth and high social position, aroused envy among the anti-Jewish fanatics—especially the clergy—who could not accept the idea of Jews holding high positions.

There had been many attempts to introduce the Inquisition into Spain, but these efforts had failed. Finally, in 1478, after Pope Sixtus IV came under of pressure from the papal nuncio, he agreed to allow King Ferdinand and Queen Isabella to appoint various archbishops and others to conduct investigations into matters dealing with the faith.

Ferdinand, enamored of the additional revenue the prosecution of "heretics" would yield, was quite willing to have the Inquisition do its work. Isabella was more reluctant, but after pressure from churchmen, she signed the decree establishing the Inquisition. This was 12 years before the Jews were expelled from Spain. The Inquisitors began their work in Seville, where they were accorded a mixed reception. The "good" Christians who had no connection with any Jews gave them a warm reception, while those who either came from Marrano stock or were intermarried with Marranos were clearly concerned about what the future might bring.

Many Marranos took refuge in Cadiz, where the Inquisition had not yet begun its work. The Inquisitors, though, sent a message to the rulers of all provinces and cities to seize all Marranos and to confiscate their property. To add impact to this message, the Inquisitors specified that anyone disobeying this edict would be excommunicated and would lose all his own property and offices. Here we see how a Catholic Church action had vast pecuniary implications for both the Marranos and for King Ferdinand, who benefited from the seizures.

As a result of this ordinance, the Marquis of Cadiz delivered 8,000 Marranos to the Inquisition in Seville. Many of the most prominent had been firmly entrenched in Spanish society. These were seized in the initial raids at the beginning of 1481. They comprised not just the wealthiest, but the most prominent and most learned municipal counselors, lawyers, and doctors.[92]

Soon the Inquisitional Tribunal began its work. It was the most hated body in Spain and aroused utter fear among all. No person was immune and no utterance was too innocent to arouse the interest of the Inquisition. And it was but a short time until the first Auto da Fé (act of faith, the practice of public burning at the stake), which took place on February 6, 1481. Six men and women, who had been accused of desecrating an image of Jesus, were the first victims. The Chief Inquisitor was present at this Auto da Fé, but was soon struck down by the plague which raged in Andalusia at that time. A few days later, three very wealthy Marranos were burned at the stake, followed by the execution of all those who had been caught in a conspiracy to resist the Inquisition.[93]

The Inquisition introduced torture machines beyond anything known before or since. Chronicles tell us that the torturers, believing they were doing God's work, had no compassion, not the slightest, for the victims. An example was a member of the Inquisition whipping a pregnant woman who was hanging upside down by her ankles. Lunch time arrived and he put down his whip and happily walked out for his meal, leaving he woman hanging.

In Seville, the Auto da Fé was a monthly event. By November of that year, more than 300 victims had been burned to death, while 79 had been tortured into confessions and, upon confessing, were sentenced to life imprisonment. Their worldly goods were confiscated.

Ferdinand gathered immense wealth from the confiscations. He was not interested in hearing how the confessions were obtained.

· 24 ·

KADDISH AND THE CONCEPT
OF DEATH

*I*N THESE PAGES we have described the persecutions of the Jews beginning in the Middle Ages. It seems clear on reflection that the *Kaddish* as a prayer of mourning was a necessary textual response to attacks instigated by the church, as well as local and national institutions in Europe over a period of several centuries, beginning with the days of the First Crusade.

Let us take a broader look at the subject. The Kaddish prayer from its inception in early rabbinic times was a method by which a Jew confirmed his belief in God. It is confirmation of God's unquestioned greatness. Its placement at different places in Jewish prayer, in different holiday seasons, its specific times, reflects the fact that no matter what the conflict (and humanity equals conflict), or what the season of the year, such as weather or drought, etc., the *Kaddish* recital confirms one's belief and praise of the Lord. No matter what, God's judgment is unquestioned.

According to most sources, the *Kaddish* began in early rabbinic times as a kind of brief meditation carrying a message of hope, a sanctification of one's belief in, and praise of, God. The prayer became formalized, then, as an element of the liturgy. Finally, after the atrocities and expulsions of the Middle Ages and beyond, the lamentation (*kinot*) and penitential prayers (*Selichot*)[94] became a strong and bitter wail of the tortured. And the ancient words of the *Kaddish* were taken up as a prayer for the dead.

And now, our study of *Kaddish* as a religious text, as well as its sources in Jewish history and tradition, must lead inevitably to a consideration of Jewish responses to the concept of death.

One could conclude that the *Kaddish* is a metaphor for many aspects of Jewishness as well as a Jewish approach to end-of-life issues. In developing this concept, there is first of all, the huge importance of the *Kaddish* as a communal tool. The fact that the *Kaddish* is recited in the company of ten persons (*minyan*) is in itself a condition for the creation of a nucleus of a community, a primary social cell.

Rabbi Akiva (in *Masechet Kallah Rabati*) ruled that the *Kaddish* is recited to elevate the soul of the dead, a fact that has merged into socio-communal customs like the *shiva*, the *Shloshim*, and the *Yahrzeit* as well as additional customs (drawn from the book of Job) which became obligatory laws declared by an eternal rabbinical authority.

Because of the importance of the Community (the *Kehila*)—the supportive environment—one begins to understand why death is not mentioned in the *Kaddish*, though it occupies the central place in funerals and their accompanying prayers.

This main issue is joined with the issue of charity and giving (*Zedaka Tazil Mi'mavet*—charity will save from death) which is not obligatory in the *Yizkor* prayers where the person who remembers does not commit himself to give charity for the elevation of souls of his dead loved ones, charity [*Gemilut Hasadim*] being one of the central pillars of the Jewish Community.)[95]

The funeral itself is one of the *mitzvot* and is considered to be part of the charity *mitzvah* since it carries with it a respect for the dead and the living (the family and friends). It is considered to be exalted since the participant does not expect to get a reward from the dead person and this is why the *Hevra Kadisha*[96] is called *"Gemilut Hasadim shel Emeth"*— a genuine charity.

Why genuine? Because at the funeral you do the *mitzvah* out of genuine altruism and not for a reward, which is why everyone who sees a funeral must participate in it. Again this is an important act of socialization, a function so important to the Jewish tradition.

There are three pillars in Jewish society: The synagogue, *Beit Hamidrash*,[97] and the *Beit Hadin*[98]—three pillars without which a Jewish community cannot be developed.

The synagogue is designated for public prayer but also for congregating and debating important issues and sometimes as a school or a *Beit Midrash*. The synagogue is a holy place and one is forbidden to defame it.

A *Beit Hamidrash* is designated for the study of the Torah. It too is holy and the students can use it for their needs since they occupy it at times all day and night. The *Beit Hadin*, a courthouse, in effect, is the place where social and personal laws and rules of life of the community were designated.

The synagogue and the *Beit Hamidrash* are conditional to the existence of Jewish life and both are necessary by consent and communal agreement. And the constant presence of the *Kaddish* in both institutions is a way to attach the whole environment to the memory of the dead, and help those left behind.

· 25 ·

THE NATURE OF DEATH

*T*HE DEATH OF our mothers—Saul's a number of years ago and mine more recently—was the inspiration for our writing this book. We sought to examine the nature of death, the end of life as perceived by Judaism—and primarily the intersection between one's loss and the *Kaddish* prayer, which I recited daily during the months following my mother's funeral.

It is possible to explore the relationship between ideas in regard to the cessation of life and the interface between life and death. How does Judaism deal with the personal trauma of death? What does Judaism demand of those who remain alive?

There are many comments and opinions about this subject,

and from many directions. We have tried to illuminate some of these in this work. And there are some fascinating studies concerning the issue, both Biblically and anecdotally, as well as in the rules and stipulations known as the *aggadah*.

Jerusalem throws out an interesting lifeline: the ideas of the World to Come and the revival of the dead. The existence of the two does not decrease by even an iota our duty in this world to perfect creation and to rectify wrongs. The Torah and the Prophets teach us what to do here and now, and are less concerned about what happens in the World to Come.

Chaim Nachman Bialik,[99] Israel's national poet, composed a seemingly innocuous children's poem: "Who is above and who below? Just I, I and you." Thousands of mothers sing this to their children as they rock back and forth on a see-saw in a local playground. Bialik, however, was referring to a verse: "What is above and what is below, what is in front and what is behind."

It is precisely these questions which Judaism forbids one to ask. Judaism encourages parents to bless their children, and Moses blessed the Children of Israel before his death, all relating to this world in spite of the fact that the basic premise relating to reward and punishment refers to the World to Come.

Contrary to this, Christianity encourages its followers to investigate "what is above and what is below." Sermons in churches often deal with death and life in the hereafter. The Jewish system of Commandments, on the other hand, lays its emphasis on "that you shall live by [the commandments] and not die by them" (*Yoma* 85), in the here and now, and with the punishment for disobeying the Commandments being given as exile.

Even eternity, the vision of the End of Days and the

messianic era will take place in this world. Man's obligation toward God is in this world: "It is not in heaven ... not across the ocean ... for this matter is very close to you. It is within your mouth and heart to do."

Thus, one may assume that Judaism does not demand asceticism or depriving oneself of the pleasures of this world (and certainly not to go to an extreme in this). Judaism is opposed to cutting oneself off from the world or from one's community. There is a belief that one's prayer should ideally be recited with a quorum of ten. In Psalms we are told that "the earth was given to mankind," and "mankind" means involvement with others.

Living in a community, observance of the Commandments relate to man's dealings with his fellow-man. The Jewish religion tells us that one who fails in this regard cannot gain atonement for his sins on Yom Kippur, for sins between man and his fellow-man are more grievous than those between man and God.

Judaism asks that the Jew act as part of the collective: that he give charity, that he help the unfortunate, that he support the persecuted. It does not desire that one should deprive himself, but rather that one should enjoy the world.

Chassidism, for example, raises joy to be the highest level of all in the perfect worship of God. Through joy, one is able to break down walls. One fasts on Yom Kippur, but it is nevertheless considered a festive day. It is a festival on which one lights festive candles and recites a blessing thanking God for "preserving us to this day."

Not only is the Chassidic Jew required to be joyful, but he is required to bring joy to others ("you shall rejoice in your festivals, you and your son and your daughter and the male and female slaves within your gates"—Deuteronomy 16:17). On the Sabbath and on festivals one is forbidden to mourn.

After a man marries, he is forbidden to enlist into the army in Israel for one year. He must remain home in order to fulfill the commandment of "making happy the wife whom he took" (Deuteronomy 24:5). Speaking of joy, the Talmudic Sage Rabbah[98] would cause merriment among his students and *Rambam* notes that they would tell jokes when the students became too tired to concentrate.

We find also that Miriam and Deborah the Prophet sang. The former after the people had crossed the Sea of Reeds. All of Psalms is a single massive song, and its composer, King David, danced and gamboled before the Lord. The Levites were singers in the Temple, and indeed the entire Bible is set to musical notes, the so-called *trope*.

The joy contained in Judaism surfaced against the prosaic life of the Jew. It enabled the Jewish masses in their villages, working in agriculture or other forms of manual labor, and who feared they could never become knowledgeable in Torah studies, to stave off despair. It was this philosophy with its message of always serving God joyfully which brought His followers relief from their anxiety and offered them hope.

Joy nurtured by inner harmony and contentment leads to a love of God and to unity among the Jewish people and will ultimately hasten the coming of redemption.

Thus, we may conclude that one of the principles of Judaism is to seek joy in this world. As to the future world (the World to Come) and the revival of the dead, there is the following thought: Such a world is one of souls, not of bodies, and is totally devoid of anything material. According to the Midrash, there is no food or drink, no procreation, no business, and no envy or hatred.

We are given an idealistic picture of the righteous sitting, their crowns on their heads, basking in the radiance of the Divine Presence. God wishes to strengthen our belief in the revival of the dead and in our ultimate redemption, and it is for this reason that He had the prophet envision the dry bones coming back to life. But our sources are very scant as far as what that world is like.

What we are taught is that our soul, the good part within us, does not die, nor does the body disappear. It decomposes into parts which assume other forms of existence.

Mourning is troublesome. I commented that the death of my mother left me with a sense of tremendous loss and overwhelming sadness. I am constantly thinking about my relationship with her, and trying to come to grips with the fact that she has been lost to this world forever. That is why it was important for me, and equally important for all of those who have lost a loved one, to attempt to understand what the future has in store.

The primary question remains: What happens when life has run its course? It is not only mourners who face the complex issue of life after death but also friends and community members who try to console the mourner. Every death presents such questions, and the following paragraphs offer answers from a traditional Jewish point of view.

Jewish religious philosophers suggest that there is a sharp difference between the body and the soul. Some say the body is limited, and is restricted to a specific place and time, while the soul can sweep about from one place to another and from one time to another, crossing all borders, all fences and walls.

The place where all souls come in contact with each other is in the World to Come, and it is there that the souls realize that the Divine spark in each of us cannot die. The souls "continue" with the tasks imposed upon them by the Creator, and if the tasks are carried out properly the souls bask in the radiance of the Divine Presence. They are now in an environment totally spiritual and devoid of any corporeal dimension.

The souls in the World to Come all unite with the souls of the righteous of all the previous generations, and together they all wait, in a world which is totally good, for those who continue in their ways in the corporeal world.

No date has been given for when the revival of the dead is to take place. Some sages claim it will occur at an earlier time and others that it will be at a later time, but all link it to the End of Days and the coming of the Messiah. The vision of the dry bones in Ezekiel appears as a model of the revival of the Jewish people and its complete redemption. Sabbath morning prayers offer the words: "There is none like You in this world and none except You in the life of the World to Come. There is none beside You, our Redeemer, in the time of the Messiah, and none who can compare with You, our Savior, in the revival of the dead." Thus we see a time frame here: this world, the World to Come, the days of the Messiah,[101] and finally the revival of the dead. In other words, when the world was created out of the primordial mass which follows creation, its design had already been mapped out.

The End of Days will be marked by God's existence being accepted by all nations, with eternal peace and the revival of the dead. There is thus a parallel here between the creation of the world and the perfection of creation, between the creation of man and the revival of the dead.

There are striking differences among our sages regarding the entire question. *Rambam*, relying on various *Aggadah* statements of the sages, claims that the body by its nature must lose the soul, and therefore the dead who are resurrected will return to a world that is totally good after a long period of life.

Regarding the messianic era, Rabbi Yehudah the President (Nasi), editor of the Mishnah, who lived at a time close to the founding of Christianity, believed that it would last for three generations. Others hold that the era will last for forty years, or four hundred years, or 365 years, or even 7,000 years (see *Sanhedrin* 99).

None of these views expands on what this time will be like—everything is totally unclear, just as the Creation was. Scientists posit that the universe began with a "Big Bang," but are at a total loss as to what preceded the Big Bang. By the same token, philosophers of religion pose it that man was placed here for a purpose. Thus one's obligation is to help others, to ensure justice, to foster truth and holiness, and thereby to help in bringing about acknowledgment of the kingdom of God over the entire world.

Saul contends that the entire belief in the revival of the dead was formulated to bring hope to the Jewish people. Each person wishes to leave his or her mark in the world, a mark which will remain after his or her death.

If the person did not succeed in leaving a mark, he or she has another chance, when the revival of the dead and the messianic era arrive. It is true that when death comes, one leaves the world as we know it; but this world is merely a corridor leading to the World to Come. There, all is different. As the Ba'al Shem Tov[102] theorizes, from our vantage point in this world, the stars all appear as small microscopic dots in the sky whereas in reality we know that each star is a gigantic entity, many of them far larger than our sun. Similarly, continues the Ba'al Shem Tov, there are Jews in this world who appear to be lowly and downtrodden, but in heaven their full radiance will be visible to all.

Many agree that the idea of resurrection offers comfort and a calming influence. "Death is permanent and always a shock no matter how prepared because it is the final surrendering of a connection." The physical separation is immediate, whereas the emotional separation is drawn out, takes place over a long period of time, and is painful. This is why the idea of other worlds after this one is a source of comfort.

My view is that there are many who greatly value the Jewish mourning customs, which are consistent with modern psychological processes: relating to death as an existential,[103] natural, and spontaneous act. The fact is that the mourning period is limited by Jewish law ("three days for crying, seven days for eulogizing, thirty days during which one may not shave or have a haircut, and twelve months of mourning for one's parents"). Beyond that point, Jewish law decrees quite brilliantly:

"Enough! You have no right to be more merciful than [God]." Abraham came to weep for Sarah and to mourn her; Joseph instituted a seven-day mourning period after the death of his father; I had a year of mourning for my father, and beyond that point many memories, as the most precious of all things, but there is no need to externalize it.

There is no need to become "addicted" to mourning and distress; one may not spurn life, one's creative forces, or life's pleasures. The death of one's mother does not result in the "death" of her child, but rearranges life's meaning. Life is felt more deeply, it is more serious, one has a greater sense of responsibility, and most of all, the mourning is internalized.

However, one is not permitted to mourn beyond the allotted time. The duty of the individual is to return to one's normal and natural life style.

Saul continued his review of the early rabbis' commentaries on the subject of death, and the following reflects that study, beginning with this key theme: "In Judaism, death is regarded as punishment for the original sin of Adam and Eve, from which it was decreed that those who come from dust will return to dust."

Death really is a departure from the natural course of events, and the Midrash holds that had Adam and Eve not sinned, man would have lived forever. However, Saul also holds that as Jewish philosophical thought developed, death began to be regarded as man's returning to his essence, completing a cycle when he dies. Thus, according to Ecclesiastes, when one dies the soul returns to God, from whence it came.

It is God who rules over death, and death has no independent existence. Compared to God, man is insignificant and the same may be said about him in relationship to the forces of nature. Man is unable to predict the date of his death, therefore one must constantly repent one's sins.

A related subject is touched on. Even though embalming is mentioned in the Torah (as we see with Jacob), among the Jewish people there has never been a funeral cult, as in other religions, where sacrifices were offered to and for the dead. Life goes on after the funeral. It is the life of the family which survives death, and not the embalmed body of a departed person.

Rabbi Yochanan claims that death was decreed upon the

wicked because they cause anger in Heaven. With the righteous, on the other hand, who contend with evil temptation throughout their lives, death means that there is no longer a need to struggle against it. Thus death becomes a component in a system of reward and punishment.

When the Torah was given at Mount Sinai, the Jews had the opportunity to return fully to God and to eliminate death, but after they sinned with the Golden Calf, death was reinstituted. Just as with Adam and Eve; first there was the sin and then death was decreed.

Gradually, the view was formulated among early *Tanna'im*,[104] rabbinic authorities, that while death is indeed a punishment, it is part of the nature of creation and of the world, and there is no way to escape it. Thus, it is quite possible for a person to die without having sinned.

Death is regarded by our sages as an aspect of the atonement for one's sins, and if a person, for example, committed the grievous sin of profaning heaven's name, when he repents, that and the very day of Yom Kippur absolve one-third of the punishment, the suffering which he endures absolves another third, and the person's death wipes away the last third.

Rabbi Yehudah adds that the day of one's death is like repentance, and it absolves one in the same way.

Rabbi Yehudah the Exilarch also holds that the day of one's death acts as atonement, and that is why we do not have to impose any of the death penalties which the Torah ordains. This is partly a result of the fact that when the Holy Temple was destroyed, the possibility of bringing a sacrifice to expiate a sin no longer existed.

How does one present oneself in heaven after death? Is there a fork in the road, with one road leading to the Garden

of Eden and the other to Gehinom? We are told that Rabbi
Yochanan wept as he was dying, and when his disciples asked
him why, he said that he was at that fork in the road, and
didn't know in which direction he would be sent. How, then,
could he not cry? (*Berachot* 41b).

Akabya ben Mehalalel said that the individual, both body
and soul, appears before the Holy Throne, and is judged based
on his deeds. Both the School of Hillel and the School of
Shammai share that belief. After being judged, the righteous
are granted eternal life while the wicked are sentenced to
twelve months in Gehinom.

Both the bodies and souls are buried. Rabbi Eliezer depicts
how the angels greet a righteous person who died and recites
to him verses related to peace. The wicked, on the other hand,
are greeted by destructive angels, who recite verses of rebuke.

An opposing view holds that the soul is independent, and
when the body is buried the soul is totally detached from it.
When the souls ascend, they find shelter underneath the
Throne of Glory, where all souls reside. Another view has all
the souls going to a place in the highest of the heavens, and
it is there that the heavenly verdict is rendered. Still another
version has it that those souls which are neither righteous nor
wicked are sent to a place administered by the angel Duma,
where, unlike the wicked, they will find rest.

According to the view that the soul leaves the body, this
occurs twelve months after the person's death, by which time
the body has decomposed. The soul ascends, not to return to
the body, as it has done during the twelve months. Indeed, the
Kaddish said by the children helps the soul to ascend.

This dichotomy regarding what happens after death is
visualized by our sages in terms of various allegories. Rabbi

Yochanan ben Zakkai describes it as a feast tendered by a king for his subjects. No one, though, knows when the feast is to begin. The more intelligent ones put on their best clothes to wait at the palace gates, ready for the feast to begin. The fools go about their regular business, and when the king proclaims that the feast is ready to be served, the intelligent enter, dressed in their best, while the fools charge in, still in their dirty clothes. The intelligent enjoy the feast thoroughly, while the foolish feel uncomfortable even sitting down to eat, and end up hungry.

Regarding another *Tanna* of the era of Rabbi Yochanan ben Zakkai,[105] Rabbi Chanina ben Dossa, we are told that his wife asked him to pray to God to receive, in this world, a little of the reward reserved for them in the World to Come. God accepted his prayer and a leg of a table made of pure gold came down to him from heaven. That night, Rabbi Chanina ben Dossa dreamed that all the other sages were dining on tables with three legs, but his table had only two. He begged God to take back the table leg, and the leg was taken back. From this story, we can see that one is not rewarded for his deeds in this world, but the reward is reserved for the World to Come.

In general, our sages tended to believe that the reward of the righteous is in the World to Come, and in that way they answered the conundrum of how one finds those who are wicked, living a life of luxury while there are many righteous ones who live a life of misery. On the other hand, there are sins that are punished in this world, as appropriate punishment fitting the crime.

The sect known as the Sadducees did not believe in reward and punishment in the World to Come, and cynically railed against the Pharisees who inflicted misery and suffering in this world, with the idea that they would receive their true reward in the World to Come.

According to the Sadducces, "Over there, there is nothing." Indeed there were many crises of faith suffered by the Pharisees when those who kept the Commandments were the ones to be punished, as seen, in the decrees of Emperor Hadrian following the crushing of Bar Kochba's revolt.

Rabbi Natan asked: "The Jewish people live in the Land of Israel, offer their lives to perform the Commandments, and are tortured and killed in the most barbaric way. If a person circumcised his son, he would be put to death. If he read the Torah, he might be burned alive. One who ate *matzah* might be crucified for doing so. If one recited the blessing on a *lulav* he might receive a hundred lashes with an iron bar."

Whenever the Jewish people faced a crisis, there were wise men who explained the varied mechanism involved in terms of reward and punishment. Such was the case after the Bar Kochba revolt failed. Rabbi Yishmael and Rabbi Shimon were both sentenced to be executed, and Rabbi Shimon asked Rabbi Yishmael why this was to happen.

Rabbi Yishmael explained that if a person came before him in judgment and he delayed the case until he finished drinking his beverage or tied his shoe, he would be contradicting the Torah commandment not to delay judgment.

Hearing this, Rabbi Shimon said, "You have comforted me."

Rabbi Akiva, who was killed by the Romans, refused to accept that explanation. To him, death was not a punishment; it was a reward. When he was tortured, he convinced himself that he must accept suffering in love. Indeed, one must love God "even if they take your life from you."

After his death, which had been preceded by terrible and

prolonged torture, our wise men said: "Rabbi Akiva was not put to death for theft or because he did not devote himself totally to Torah study. He was killed as a sign"—i.e., for the Torah ideal, for the continuation of the life force of the Jewish people. He was granted the privilege of dying to sanctify God's name, and that is why he is venerated.

Accepting this concept, one can understand how one can have free will, can choose how one wants to act, with all the consequences of his decisions, and at the same time know that in the final analysis the balance of reward and punishment will be maintained. One who deserves it will be privileged to die in the most exalted of all ways, the death of the righteous.

That justifies Rabbi Akiva's view that while all is planned in advance, one nevertheless has the option to choose what course to take, with the knowledge that in the final analysis one will have to account for his deeds and misdeeds. This also explains the saying that if a person observes a single commandment, his life is extended. It also explains the statement by Rabbi Tarfon that "Your Employer (i.e., God) can be trusted to pay your wages for your actions," not here, but in the World to Come. The reward for one's good deeds is reserved for the World to Come.[106]

One has freedom of choice in this world, and each choice defines one's fate in the World to Come.

When a person thinks of reward and punishment, one must emphasize the value of pure ethics. Those who serve God only so they will be rewarded for doing so are not the role models to follow. It is a mistake to serve God and perform His commandments only because of fear of Him and His punishments.

There is not an automatic mechanism of reward and punishment in this world. When we turn to the Book of Job, we learn not to repeat the mistakes of Job's friends, and not to attempt to try to understand how God rules the world. One cannot decide *a priori* that everyone who is doing well in our society is a good person and everyone who is in trouble is bad. That is a simplistic approach that presumes we can understand God's bookkeeping.

"Life is like this fine china," says Saul. "It is fragile, but contains within itself much beauty and goodness." Feelings like this enrich our lives. We recall that in conversations with middle-aged friends who are deeply devoted to their careers, questions rise about the purpose of life. If there is no purpose, no goal, and no mission; there is no reason to live. You are simply spinning your wheels. You are studying in order to get a better job, and with that you will be able to buy food so that you can have the strength to eat, so that you can work.

From time to time you manage to see a good play, dine in a fine restaurant, obtain spiritual satisfaction from a concert, book, or lecture. Then that passes and you are back to the familiar treadmill. If one has no purpose in life, the only thing that one can relate to is the fact that "I am alive." If our life has no purpose beyond itself, then there is nothing beyond the grave. Then all of one's existence is here, in this world, a very short moment in the eternity of the earth.

What is the purpose of all of my labor and effort, if the only thing that exists is my body? It follows that the only thing that one should do with his life is enjoy it to the fullest, to live hedonistically: 'Eat, drink, and be merry, for tomorrow we die."

There are no pockets in a shroud and after death, there is

no longer a living body, there is no longer existence. There is no future and there is no significance to life. Thoughts such as these can fill a person with despair. If all I am is what I am now, my body, and after I die all will vanish, isn't it crazy not to pamper my ego, myself?

The skeptic asks himself: "Why should I be concerned about others, who are concerned only about themselves, by sacrificing that which I possess? Everyone, including one's own children, should fend for themselves."

Every human being has a function in this world. It is to fulfill a function for which each creature was created. If one fulfills one's function, life is justified. That is why one has no right to flee from the world. Our world was created so that each individual would fulfill his destiny. Thus, God imparted into each body the physical and biological ability to advance spiritually, to change, to move beyond a starting point and reach for and achieve goals.

When a person fulfills his destiny and his soul gains supremacy over his body, using his body to fulfill God's commands, our sages tell us that then the body can truly end its function in the world and come to rest, while the soul will return to its place and enjoy the perfection to be achieved in its rightful Place on High.

It is night time and I am about to recite the last *Kaddish* for my mother in a Manhattan synagogue. We are almost at the end of our journey and our intense quest to explore Judaism and the *Kaddish*.

We have come away with new insights, the most important being a better understanding of *Kaddish*, how it grew and why we say it for the departed.

On our journey, we found the connection between *Kaddish*

and death and mourning. We are better able to understand the rituals of the funeral and the year after the death, a connection which was historically only made during the Crusades and the Black Death.

It became clear to us that much of religion and religious practices are trans-cultural. We wonder why there has been so much conflict, and so much hate and distrust among people who have different ways to worship God. This is one of the great unanswered questions of life.

*H*ow did the *Kaddish* become the most famous and familiar prayer in Jewish liturgical doxology? We know now that to understand the meaning of *Kaddish*, one must have a modest understanding of Jewish history.

It seems to the authors that perhaps the history of the *Kaddish* exemplifies the brilliant elasticity of Judaism and how it was modified in certain fundamental ways by the scholars and rabbis in order to fill the spiritual needs of all its people.

We were not able to find a specific author of the Mourner's *Kaddish*. However, the question remains: Should a Jew say *Kaddish*, and if so, why?

If one is a follower of Orthodox Judaism there is no question but that one is required to say the *Kaddish* three times daily for eleven or twelve months. Among Conservative or Reform Jews, the commitment may be less.

Whatever branch of Judaism one follows, it is clear that the saying of *Kaddish* has become a mainstay of Judaism. It is impossible to have a Jewish burial without *Kaddish*. This is so because the saying of *Kaddish* relates to the basic concept of community in Judaism.

Then there is also the requirement that *Kaddish* be said within a *minyan*, and so reinforcing the concept of "community"—fundamental in Judaism and Judaic history.

May one say *Kaddish* alone? The answer is no.

The rabbis assert that it is unhealthy to grieve alone—for psychological reasons. Historically, as we have seen in this book, rabbinical Judaism is really about enforcing the concept of community. The *Kaddish* with a *minyan* creates a sense of group therapy for the mourners and a bonding.[107]

When *Kaddish* is recited in the synagogue, it is customary for all those who say *Kaddish* to speak in unison. This creates a bonding and a mutuality of mourning and grief-sharing.

Great rabbis had wonderful insight into human nature and the human psyche, and discerned ways to preserve the religion of the Jews, a religion that, realistically, had passed away many centuries before, when the Second Temple was destroyed.[108]

The early rabbis had the power of wisdom, and with that power they became the leaders of the Jewish people. The leadership passed to the rabbis from the priests, who were the leaders of the community by virtue of their service and status in caring for the holy temple. Once the temple was destroyed, the priests lost their power.

Although there were other synagogues in Israel at the

time of the destruction of the Second Temple, the holy temple in Jerusalem was the main citadel of prayer and religious ritual. It was the vortex of the Jewish people. Once the temple was destroyed, the rabbis became leaders of the Jews.[109] They exported Judaism from Israel to other countries throughout the world, establishing synagogues and Judaism in the Diaspora.

This was one of the great phenomena in world history. The rabbis kept the Jewish religion alive for centuries. It outlasted all the other major cultures of the world, and especially the Greeks and Roman. Synagogues became a place of prayer and a center of study and community. It was the reciting of *Kaddish* in a *minyan* that fostered and reinforced the communal aspects of Judaism.

Although the sources of the *Kaddish* prayer remain obscure, it became an invaluable spoke in the wheel of Judaism and the oil that helped keep the Jews in tradition and kept the religion alive.

Perhaps the fact that it is so mysterious is what makes the *Kaddish* fascinating and important. It is truly enigmatic and profound, creating a spirituality whether one is a practicing Jew or not.

From the early days of the giving of the torah to the present, wherever conflict arose between literal obscure religious doctrine and statements which were incomprehensible or admittedly incapable of literal observance, rabbinical Judaism brilliantly created avenues of relief. These were within the Jewish framework and allowed the religion to survive and flourish.

The *Kaddish* prayer and ritual is an affirmation of such brilliance and faith. This in the author's opinion, will keep Judaism alive and vibrant for eternity.

GLOSSARY

ARAMAIC—A northern Semitic language closely related to Hebrew which served as the official language of the Ancient Persian Empire. It is mentioned in the Bible as a language understood by the leaders of Judea already in the time of First Temple. During the Second Temple the Jews returning from Babylonia brought the Aramaic to Eretz-Israel and since then it has become the trade and official language in the country, ousting the Hebrew language from the towns. From the Aramaic evolved the square Hebrew script which eventually replaced the ancient Hebrew script. The Babylonian Talmud is written in an Eastern dialect of Aramaic while the Talmud Yerushalmi (Palestinian) in a Western dialect. Aramaic penetrated the liturgy: The *Kaddish*, the *Kol Nidrey* and the opening of the Passover Haggadah are in Aramaic. Aramaic is still spoken in various communities.

ASSERET HARUGEY MALCHUT (10 MARTYRS)—Ten leading Jewish Sages who were executed after torture by the Romans, most of them in the time of Hadrian's decrees because they taught the Torah in public

ASHKENAZI COMMUNITIES—From the mid 9th century—*Gaonic* period—the name Ashkenaz became identified with Germany. Jewish communal and social life as well as Jewish scholarship developed in Christian Europe from the three Rhineland communities of Spire, Worms, and Mainz in the 10th century thence they spread westward to France through Rashi and his descendants and eastward to Germany and Bohemia, establishing a unity of custom. Ashkenazi ritual and law differed from the parallel tradition developing in what was then Moslem Europe—Spain. As a result the word Ashkenaz became applied to a religious and cultural tradition of those who followed the custom which originated among German Jews. With the drift of German Jews over the eastern borders of their country into the Slavonic lands in the 16th century and the adoption by the Jews in those countries of the traditions and language, namely Yiddish of the German Jews, the word Ashkenaz received an even wider connotation.

AV HA'RACHAMIM ("MERCIFUL FATHER")—Martyrs' memorial dirge; probably composed after the Crusaders massacres of 1096, influenced by the Ritual of the non-Jews.

BA'AL SHEM TOV (HA-BESHT), RABBI ISRAEL—(1700–1760). Founder of the Chassidic Movement. Born in the Ukraine to a poor family and became an orphan at an early age. As a young man he traveled through small towns, healing the sick with herbs and amulets. After his marriage he retired to solitude and meditation in the woods in Podolia. He felt he had a mission to stir the hearts of those seeking communion with God. This was done through praying while trembling. The emphasis on "intention" (*kavanah*) was a further basic tenet of the Besht. True prayer was pictured as a state which freed the personality from the trammels of the body and allowed fusion of the soul with God. He received his name because of good deeds to the poor. Shem Tov literally means "good name" in Hebrew.

BABYLONIAN TALMUD —See Talmud.

BAR-KOKHVA—Leader of the rebellion against the Romans in the years 132–5 C.E. Many, including Rabbi Akiva, thought he was the Messiah King (Chazall denied this and called him Bar Koziva—liar). For a short while the Jews liberated Judea and Bar Kokhva served as the president. However, the Romans mobilized large troops from far off and defeated Bar Kokhva's army. The Romans wanted to annul the national uniqueness of the Jews and therefore prohibited the study of the Torah, the gathering in synagogues, and the celebration of Sabbath and holidays. Almost everybody continued to observe the *mizvot* in secrecy, and the braver ones in the open, but those who were caught became martyrs.

BEGIN, MENACHEM—The sixth Prime Minister of Israel in the years 1977–1983, when he resigned due to bad health. In 1948 the set up the "Cherut" (Liberation) Party which was the largest party of the opposition until he became Prime Minister in 1977. Before the establishment of the State of Israel Begin was Head of the "*Etzel*" (*Irgun Tzeva'I Le'umi*), a clandestine military group fighting the British rule in Palestine.

BELZ—Town in Galicia; original seat of the Chassidic dynasty of the Rokeach family, established by Shalom of Belz (1799–1855). The Belz rebbis laid great stress on rabbinic learning and were very extreme in their insistence on a specific Jewish appearance, any diminution of which diminished the "Divine Image" in which man was created. They had a great influence on the development of Galician Chassidism. The present rebbe's seat is now in Jerusalem and he has thousands of *chassidim* (followers).

BEIT DIN—[Heb. "house of judgment, court"]: Jewish court of law guided by the principles of the official *halachah* in dealing with matters of civil, criminal or religious law. The judges received their authorization from the heads of the *yeshivot* or from the Patriarch. A higher court consisted of 23 judges and was empowered to judge criminal cases and was called some times "small Sanhedrin." The highest type of court was known as the Great Beit Din or Sanhedrin.

BEIT HAMIDRASH—[Heb. "house of study"]: Place for study of the Law, and, more specifically, of the rabbinic texts such as the Mishnah, Talmud, Codes, and Responsa. In the Talmudic Period, the term *Beit Hamidrash* was almost synonymous with that of *yeshiva*. Its sanctity was considered greater than that of the synagogue and rabbis of the Talmud preferred to pray there rather than adjourning to the synagogue. During medieval times it became close to the *Bet Knesset* (Synagogue) usually situated in the same building or close by. In Eastern Europe it was termed *kloize*. It was here that senior students would spend most of their day either in individual study or under the discipline of a *Rosh Yeshiva*.

BEIT (SCHOOL OF) HILLEL AND BEIT SHAMMAI—Two schools of *tannaim* (the last of the pairs of *tannaim*) flourishing in the 1st century C.E. The Talmud records more than 300 controversies on points of law between the two schools. The Shammaite school was strict and uncompromising, while the Hillel school was kind and gentle.

BETH-LEHEM—The native town of King David (and birthplace of Jesus] and the burial place of Rachel *Imenu* (Heb. "our Mother").

BEN-GURION, DAVID—(1886–1973). The first Prime Minister of Israel. A man of great vision and wisdom. It is said of him that without him the State of Israel would not have been established. He devoted his life to the establishment and the shaping of the State of Israel. Among his great achievements are the creation of the Israeli Army (*Tzahal*) the German Reparations Agreement, the establishment of the State Schooling system, and many many others. In 1963 he retired from all political activity and settled in a kibbutz in the Negev to write his history.

BIALIK, CHAIM NACHMAN—(1873–1934). The greatest Jewish poet in modern times, known as the national poet. Born to a poor family in Russia and from the age of seven, after his father's death, was raised by his grandfather. He studied in a Yeshiva but left it at the age of 18 and went to Odessa, where he lived till 1921 and published his first poetry book. Following the Kishinev Riots he wrote his famous poems "On the Slaughter" (*Al Hashkhita*) and "At the Slaughter Town" (*Be'ir Ha-Hareiga*). His poems shattered the Jewish world and urged it to organize protection. In 1924 he emigrated to Palestine and lived in Tel-Aviv, where he became a central and most popular cultural figure.

BLACK PLAGUE—The Bubonic Plague which broke out in Europe in 1347 rapidly spreading and killing half of its inhabitants. The Black Death, as it was called, was doubly hard on the Jews, who not only died of it like the gentiles, but were also accused of causing the disease. As a result, 210 Jewish communities in Europe were completely destroyed and many others were deserted. The remaining Jews wandered into Poland and Lithuania where the plague did not reach as many regions. But the disaster had positive results too: the widespread death contributed to the technological development needed to overcome the lack of workers, also a lot of money remained after the death of so many people and helped give rise to capitalism. And in the Jewish world, Yiddish, the language of the German Jews, moved on with them to Eastern Europe.

BLOOD LIBEL—The worst libel from which the Jews have suffered in the Diaspora. They were accused of murdering Christian children and using their blood for the preparation of the Passover *matzah* and the four glasses of wine of the Seder night. Following the Blood Libel the accused were tried by a mock court which incited the mob to riot. There was also Blood Libel in the background of anti-Semitic events like the Dreyfus trial in France.

CANAAN; LAND OF CANAAN—the ancient name of the area of southern Syria and Palestine. In The Bible, Canaan is the name of one of Ham's sons, grandson of Noah. According to the Bible, the land of Canaan was promised to Abraham and his descendents.

CHAFETZ CHAIM—The denomination (after the name of his first book) of Rabbi Israel Meir Hacohen (1838–1933) whose home in Lithuania was named "The Radin Yeshiva." An exemplary figure of a decider and moralist who is also known for his battle against bad language.

CHALLOT—The white flour loaves of bread prepared for Sabbath and festive meals.

CHASSIDIC—Belonging to the Chassidut Movement (Chassidism), a religious and social movement established by the Rabbi Israel Baal Shem-Tov around 1700 among the Jews in the Ukraine and Podolia, spreading later on into other Eastern European countries. Nowadays found mainly in Israel and in the USA, and lately has become worldwide. The main novelty of the Chassidut movement was its emphasis on the idea that everyone, whether a scholar or ignorant can become a "Chassid"—a person of great piety and fervor and therefore a favorite of God, if only he will keep directing his thought to the love of God and accept the instructive authority of the *Tzaddik* (leader of the congregation).

CHATZI KADDISH—(Heb. Half of the *Kaddish*, i.e. the first half) It is recited by the *chazan* (cantor) in the morning prayer (*Shacharit*) before "*Barchu*" and after the standing prayer, and in the afternoon (*Mincha*) and evening (*Arvit*) prayers before the standing prayer. It is also recited after the reading of the Torah.

CHAZAN—Cantor. Originally the term denoted a community official carrying out a variety of functions. In the course of time emphasis was laid almost exclusively on voice quality.

CHEVRA KADDISHA—(Heb. and Aram.: "holy association) Applies to the "brotherhood" of men which undertakes to perform the religious task of the burying of the dead according to the Jewish Law which is a sacred, voluntary duty.

CHIDDUSHEI HA'RIM—A work written by the Rebbe of Gur—Isaac Meir Alter. Chiddushim is *novellae*—a customary designation of certain talmudic commentary.

CHIEF RABBINATE—The supreme religious institution in Israel. The Rabbinate consists of 24 rabbis—12 Ashkenazi, 12 Sephardi, and of course two Chief Rabbis, one of each community.

Established in 1921 with Rabbi Avraham Yitzhak Hacohen Kook and Rabbi Uziel.

COHEN—[Heb. "priest"] The male descendants of Aharon from the tribe of Levi were endowed with the hereditary functions, responsibilities, and privileges of the priestly office. From all past prohibitions there remain today the prohibition to marry a divorcee, a harlot, or a woman born of an illicit priestly marriage, or defile himself by contact with a corpse or even enter a cemetery.

CONSERVATIVISM—A religious movement which developed in the U.S. in the 20th century, inspired by the 19th century. The movement maintains that both the Written Torah and the Oral Torah must be observed but with flexibility adapted to the changing times. It promotes tolerance and distancing from extremism.

DAF YOMI—(Heb. "daily page") Initiated by Rabbi Meir Shapiro from Lublin in 1923, the Talmud Bavli is studied all over the world in the exact same order—i.e, a page a day. The counting began on Rosh Hashana 1924, and a whole cycle of the Talmud reading takes seven and a half years to finish. That way every Jew, wherever he is, can join the learning of the Talmud without missing a page. This practice is flourishing again in Israel and in the Diaspora.

EICHMANN, ADOLF—(1906–1962) One of the chief bureaucrats of the Nazi regime and the supervisor of the "Final Solution" plan to exterminate the Jews. He escaped to Argentina and was caught by Israeli Mossad agents and brought to Israel to be tried. His trial was a public one broadcast on the radio. He was found guilty and was hanged on May 31, 1962.

EVIL EYE—("A grudging eye") A widespread and still extant superstition that the malignant and envious eye of an ill-disposed person can cause harm. Formulae were drawn up to be said in times of prosperity in order to ward off any evil eye (cf. the Yiddish phrase *kainehora, "without an evil eye"*).

GA'ON—The denomination of the Heads of the Babylonian

Yeshivot—Sura and Pumbedita (600–1040).The *Ga'onim* were actually the spiritual leaders of all the Diaspora at the time.

GARDEN OF EDEN—In the Torah, the garden where Adam and Eve lived before they tasted the fruit of the Tree of Knowledge and were expelled from it. In the Talmud and later literature this is the abode of the "pious" souls where they are rewarded for their good deeds.

GEHINOM—The place of punishment for the souls of the sinful after their death, named after the valley outside the western wall of Jerusalem which served for child sacrifice to the Moloch, refuse of the city, and carcasses of animals.

GEMARA—(Aramaic tradition or studying) The usual designation for the comment on and discussions around the Mishnah. The Mishnah together with the Gemarah make up the Talmud. There is a Babylonian Gemara and a Palestinian Gemara.

GEMILUT CHASSADIM SHEL EMETH—(Heb. "bestowal of loving kindness") Any act of kindness, consideration, and benevolence. Gemilut Chassadim is unlimited in its application and is listed among those actions of which "man enjoys the fruit in this world, while the stock remains to him in the world to come." It is considered superior to almsgiving, which could humiliate the recipient. The term came to be applied more specifically to the lending of money free of interest to those in need of temporary financial assistance and Gemilut Chassadim societies exist for this purpose.

GE'ONIM, GA'ON—The title given to the Heads of the Yeshivot (academies) in Babylon: Sura and Pumbedita from the 7th century. until the decline of the Jewish center there. The denomination "*Ga'on*" (genius) denotes greatness.

GIMATRIA—Numerical value of the Hebrew letters.

GOLEM OF PRAGUE—See the *Maharal.*

GUR—See the *Rebbe of Gur.*

HA'ARI OF SAFED (THE SACRED), LURIA YITZHAK ASHKENAZI— (1537–1572). Kabbalist of Safed and founder of a new school of mysticism which exerted a profound influence on the whole

Jewish world and formed the theoretical basis for much of the late Chassidic thought. Born in Jerusalem and spent most of his life in Safed where he died, living an ascetic life with a small circle of followers. and becoming a legendary figure.

HAGGADAH—("narration") The set form in which the story of the Exodus must be told on the first two nights of Passover (in Israel, only on the first night) as part of the ritual "Seder" (*order*) of these nights.

HALACHA—(Heb. "law") That part of Jewish literature, stemming especially from the talmudic and later periods, which deals with religious, ethical, civil, and criminal law. The plural, *halachot*, is often used to refer to a collection of laws.

HAVDALAH—(Heb. "demarcation" between the holy and secular) A prayer recited at the conclusion of Sabbaths and holy festivals to indicate the distinction between the sacred day that has ended and weekday which is beginning.

HOLOCAUST MEMORIAL DAY—The Holocaust and Heroism Memorial Day is on 27 Nissan—the day the Warsaw Ghetto's Rebellion was suppressed. On this day in Israel all the entertainment places are closed and an official central memorial ceremony takes place in Yad Vashem (Holocaust, Martyrs and Heroes' Remembrance Authority).

HOMILETIC LITERATURE—The literature which interprets scripture in order to extract its full implications and meaning which usually formed a response to the need of a particular age or environment.

INQUISITION—An ecclesial court ("Holy Office") set up by the Catholic Church for the trial of heretics, i.e. those who abandoned the religious tenets and beliefs of the catholic faith in which they had been brought up or which they had adopted. Its operation was entrusted to the Dominicans. It was first exercised against the Albigenses in Southern France in the 13th century. The inquisition is best known for its relentless hunting down of the descendants of converted Jews (Marranos) in Spain in the

14th century. It lasted for 359 years from the first *auto-da-fe* in Seville in 1481 until its final abolition in 1834. It is estimated that the Spanish Inquisition sentenced from its establishment until 1808 over 30,000 Marranos to be burned at the stake, while another 16,000 were punished *in absentia*, being burnt in effigy.

ISRAELI KNESSET—The Israeli Parliament, seated in Jerusalem.

IYOV (JOB), THE BOOK OF—The third book of the Hafiographa that bears the name of Job, the hero of the story of a person of exemplary righteousness. Satan is granted a free hand to test Job's faith in God.

KABBALAH—In the 13th century the term came to be applied to the new mystical doctrines and systems that had been developing in southern France and Spain since the 12th century and which reached their literary climax in the *Book of Zohar*.

KADDISH DE'RABBANAN—In this *Kaddish* there is an additional passage, *"Al Israel ve'al Rabbanan,"* to Torah students and blessing to them.

KADDISH HA'GADOL—Recited at a burial.

KADDISH SHALEM (WHOLE)—Is recited by the *chazan* before the end of each of the three daily prayers, and is also named *"Kaddish Titkabel."*

KADDISH TITKABEL —Is the same as the *Kaddish Shalem* (whole *Kaddish*) and is so called because the *chazan* also says in it the verse *"titkabel..."* (will the prayer of Israel be accepted).

KADDISH YATOM (ORPHAN'S KADDISH)—This *Kaddish* Is recited, after the prayer, after *"aleynu le-shabe'ach,"* and *Shir shel Yom* by he who mourns his parents and relatives and he who has a *Yahrzeit*.

KATAN—[Heb. "minor"] A child who has not reached the age of 13 (a boy) and 12 (a girl) and therefore is not responsible for his/her deeds and not obliged to observe the commandments (Mitzvot). Likewise, he/she cannot participate as members of a *minyan* (see below).

KASTNER, RUDOLF—(1906–1957). An Israeli lawyer and journalist, of Rumanian origin, who during 1942–45 lived in

Budapest and was the deputy Head of the Hungarian Zionist Movement. He negotiated with the Nazis in order to liberate and save hundreds of Jews from Bergen Belsen Camp in exchange for 10,000 lorries and goods for the Germans. In 1953 he was accused by another Israeli—Malkiel Grunwald—of collaboration with the Nazis as well as giving false evidence in the Nuremberg Trials in favor of the S.S. officer Kurt Becher. He was tried and acquitted from the first accusation but was murdered by a right extremist on 15 March 1957, before the Supreme Court gave the verdict which accepted his guilt of false evidence.

KHALUTZIM (PIONEERS)—The first settlers in Eretz-Israel (Palestine) in modern time.

KIBBUTZIM—The kibbutz was an experimental communal agricultural settlement in Palestine that sought to integrate and realize in its way of life nationalist ideals with humanist-socialist ones.

KIDDUSH—Proclaims the sanctity of the Sabbath day at its beginning with a blessing of sacramental wine.

KINOT (LAMENTS)—Form of elegy recited in biblical and talmudic times in mourning over an individual or a national catastrophe.

LAG BA'OMER—A minor festival. The 33rd day of the seven-week period of the Counting of the Omer, which extends from the second day of Passover (Pesach) to Pentecost (Shavu'ot). On Lag Ba'Omer the period of semi-mourning is lifted and weddings, haircuts, etc. are permitted, the traditional reason for which is the ceasing of the plague which killed 24,000 of Rabbi Akiva's pupils. Lag Ba'Omer is also Rabbi Shimon Bar-Yohai *yahrzeit* which is celebrated by bonfires in Miron.

LECHA DODI—(Heb. "Come my beloved") A *piyut* composed in the 16th century by the Safed Kabbalist Shlomo Halevi Alkabetz and sung at the inauguration of the Sabbath,

LIUBAVICH—See the *Rebbe of Liubavich.*

MA'ARIV—Evening Service, also called A*rvit.*

MAHARAL—The denomination of Rabbi Yehuda Liva ben Bezalel, one of the greater rabbis in Europe in the 16th century.

Lived in Poland and in Prague, where he established the large Yeshiva "The Kloise." Was considered the leader of the Jewry of Ashkenaz and admired by it as an opponent of the gentile hatred of Israel. Legend has it that he built a "*golem*" (automaton) from clay and, by inserting under its tongue one of God's mystic names would cause it to become alive and do errands for the Maharal. Once he forgot to take it out of its mouth and the *golem* became a menace to the town and had to be destroyed by its creator.

MASSECHET—A Tractate of the Mishnah (hence of the Tosephta or Talmud) dealing with a specific subject and sub-divided into chapters.

MAZAL TOV—Heb. "Good luck") The formal expression of congratulations on a happy event.

MECHITZA—(Heb. "partition") A division in the synagogue separating men from women during public prayer.

MENORAH (HEB. "CANDELABRUM")—There are two candelabra of religions significance: the seven-branched *menorah* of the Temple and the later eight-branched one (with an additional socket for the "server") used at the festival of *Hanukkah*. The seven-branched *menorah* became one of the most familiar Jewish symbols.

MESSIAH—The eschatological king who is to rule over Israel at the end of days. The messianic king would destroy the enemies of Israel and establish a paradise-like reign of peace and prosperity.

MINYAN—Minimum quorum of ten adult males required for liturgical purposes such as the recital of *Kaddish*. Ten adult males constitute a representative section of the "community of Israel" for all purposes.

MIKVEH—A pool of running water containing natural (not pumped) water—i.e., spring water—serving for immersion for the purpose of purification. Today it serves mainly women who come to purify themselves from their monthly menstruation.

MISHNA—Not so much a code as a textbook, giving the essence of the Oral Law as it was known to the sages of the time. It recorded conflicting opinions and very often named the disputants. Compiled by Yehuda Hanassi (The President) by year 220 C.E.

BEN MAIMON, MOSES (MAIMONIDES OR RAMBAM)—(1135–1204) Philosopher and codifier, born in Spain but lived most of his life in Egypt, where he was physician to the court. Maimonides wrote several books. In *Mishne Torah* (Second Torah) or *Yad Hahazaka* (Strong Hand), which he wrote in Hebrew, he summed up the laws and commandments of the Torah. The book became a standard work of Jewish law and a major source for subsequent codes. Even more significant in many respects was his book *Moreh Nevuchim* (Guide for the Perplexed), in which he wrote about the principal theological problems of Judaism, a book that was written for those who follow both Torah and philosophy and who are "perplexed" by the contradictions between the teachings of the two. Naturally this book provoked a storm of Orthodox protest accusing the Rambam of (at least) encouraging heresy, but finally the name of the Rambam became established as the symbol of the pure and orthodox faith; and the inscription on his tombstone says it all: "From Moses to Moses there was none like unto Moses."

MINCHA—(Heb. "offering") The second of the two statutory daily prayers, the other being *Shakharit.*

MOUNT OF OLIVES—A mountain, considered sacred, east of Jerusalem opposite *Har Ha-Bayit* (Temple Mount) on which the Jews of Jerusalem were buried.

NE'ILAH—(Heb. "closing") The last prayer recited, with particular solemnity and to impressive melodies, on Yom Kippur (Day of Atonement) at nightfall when the fast ends.

PASSOVER (PESACH)—First of the three Pilgrim Festivals (14 Nissan), commemorating the Exodus of the children of Israel from Egypt, observed for eight days in the Diaspora and seven days in Israel and by Reform Jews. The *Seder* ceremony celebrated on the first night(s) of the festival is the most important home ceremony in the liturgical year. Special dietary laws apply to the entire duration of the festival. They are (a) the strict prohibition against eating (or keeping at home) any leaven; and (b) the commandment to eat *matzah* applies to the duration of the festival. The first and the last day of Pesach are considered holy days and all work is prohibited.

OLAM HA'BA (THE WORLD TO COME)—The concept of *Olam Ha'Ba* is different from that of Heaven or Paradise which is the abode of departed souls pending the advent of the "coming age." The *Olam Ha'Ba* designates the spiritual world to which the soul arrives after death. The belief in the *Olam Ha'Ba* is one of the principles of Judaism. In the *Olam Ha'Ba* the pious will be rewarded for their good deeds and the wicked will be punished. And the *Olam Ha'Ze* (the current empirical world) is a corridor leading to the *Olam Ha'Ba*. The Gemara says that in the *Olam Ha'Ba* there is no food and no drink, no hatred, and no envy, no negotiations and no reproduction, only *Tzaddikim* sitting with diadems on their heads enjoying the beauty of the Divine Presence.

ORTHODOXY—Modern designation for the strictly traditional section of Jewry united in their acceptance of the Divine Law in its written and oral forms, as immutable and binding for all times.

PAYTANIM—Paytan is the author of a Piyyut (a poem)—a synagogal liturgical poetry added to the statutory prayers.

PORTUGUESE SYNAGOGUE—When the expelled Spanish Jews arrived in Holland, the country was at war with Spain. As a result they called themselves Portuguese. The Jews integrated well in Holland and, among other institutions, built in 1670 their famous splendid synagogue named "The Portuguese Synagogue" in Amsterdam.

PURIM—A festival celebrated on the 14th and 15th of the month of *Adar* commemorating the deliverance of the Jews of the Persian Empire from extermination. There are four precepts in this festival: the public reading of *Megillat Esther (The Book of Esther)*,

Mishlo'akh Manot, Presents to the Poor, and *Se'udat Purim* (Purim feast). Since the Middle Ages and probably under the influence of the Christian carnivals, it became customary to disguise in fancy dress.

RABBI AKIVA (4 C.E.- 135 C.E.)—A *tanna*. Laid the foundations for the exposition of the Oral Law as later codified in the Mishnah and is credited with having arranged the Oral Law into its divisions of Mishnah, Tosephta, Siphra, and Siphrey. He is especially noted for his hermeneutic exposition of scripture, finding a basis for the Oral Law in almost every peculiarity or superfluity in the language of the Bible. His method was opposed by his great contemporary Rabbi Ishmael, who taught that "Scripture spoke in the language of men"—i.e., it must be interpreted straightforwardly and literally. He was a prime supporter of the Bar Kokhva revolt, arrested as a rebel by the Romans and imprisoned for a very long period, and finally executed after torture in Caesarea. His martyrdom became a lasting legend of exemplary love of God and faithfulness to Judaism.

RABBI ELIMELECH OF LIZHENSK—(1717–1787) His book *No'am Elimelech* is one of the foundations the Chassidism. He proposes the idea that one should believe entirely in the Tzaddik since he is the mediator between man and God and can achieve anything through his prayer.

RABBI ISERLES MOSHE (HA'RAMA)—(1525–1572) Lived in Krakow, Poland. One of the greatest last Deciders (Poskim). He added to the book of *Shulkhan Arukh*, by Joseph Karo, decisions by Ashkenazi sages, thereby converting the Sephardi book to the Law Book of the whole nation.

RABBI KOOK, AVRAHAM YITZHAK—(1865–1935) Chief Rabbi of Palestine (from 1921) and a spiritual leader whose personality, thought and writings appealed to religious and non-religious alike. He called for a Judaism which will include all the variegated expressions of the Jewish religious genius—its law, legends, poetry, mysticism, etc. Kook was inclined to see the hidden mystical streams of Jewish thought as the "soul" of Judaism, as part of the "fuller and deeper" *Torah*.

Rabbi Levi Yitzchak—(1740–1809) A Chassidic Rabbi born in the Ukraine and later settled in Berdichev in Poland, where he served as a Rabbi devoting his energy to consolidate the Hassidut Movement, educating the people to worship God in joy, devotion, and enthusiasm.

Rabbi Menachem Mendl of Kotzk—(1787–1859) A Chassidic Rabbi ("The Kotzker") was a radical and extremely critical scholar. Until the age of 40 he studied with famous Rabbis and then became a Rebbe in Kotzk. He hated mediocrity and his famous saying was, "Only horses walk in the middle of the road, human beings walk along the edges." He was extremely demanding and critical of himself and of others. He urged his pupils to seek truth and never compromise about it. His last 20 years were marked by his strange and inexplicable seclusion in a room in his own home where he shut himself up, eating a plate of soup once a day and communicating with his pupils through a hole in the door. He asked for his writings to be burnt after his death. His closest pupil was Rabbi Meir Yitchak Alter from Gur who later established his own Chassidic congregation of Gur.

Rabbi Nachman of Bratzlav—(1772–1810) One of the most original of the Chassidic leaders. A great-great-grandson of the Ba'al Shem-Tov. Regarded himself as the only true interpreter of his teachings, thus incurring the hostility of other Chassidic rabbis by his criticism of them. He stressed simple faith and prayer as against intellectualism and developed the theory of the Tzaddik as the intermediary between man and God. His outstanding contribution to Hasidic literature is his collection of folk tales (*Sippurei Ma'asiyot*)—homely parables which his followers believe to enshrine the most recondite and esoteric mysteries.

Rabbi Shimon Bar Yohai—(2nd century C.E.) *Tanna*, pupil of Rabbi Akiva. Lived and conducted his school at Teko'a in Upper Galilee. The *halachic* Midrashim, Siphrey, and Mekhilta evolved from the teachings of his Yeshiva which was noted for systematic classification of *halachot* and attempts to adduce a rational basis for the Torah. Bar Yohai had a reputation as a miracle worker. For speaking against the Romans, he was condemned to death and he and his son, Elazar, consequently went into hiding. They spent 12 to 13 years in a cave in Peki'in until the death decree was annulled. Many legends were woven around this period. Kabbalists attribute the origin of the *Book of Zohar* to this period. His traditional death date on Lag Ba'Omer is a traditional folk celebration in Miron, in the Galilee, highlighted with bonfires.

RASHI—(Abbrev. for Rabbi Shelomoh Yitzhaki—1040–1104) A French Biblical and Talmudic scholar. He founded in his native town Troyes his own Yeshiva which attracted many students. He is famous for his interpretative works. His commentaries excel all others by the lucidity and precision with which they explain even the most intricate subject. In some cases he even included interpretations from the Midrash. His commentary on the Bible was the first dated Hebrew book printed (1475) and it was translated into Latin. It was said of Rashi that but for his commentary, the Talmud would have been forgotten.

RACHEL—One of the four Matriarchs of the Nation. Rachel was the beloved wife of Jacob and the mother of Joseph and Benjamin, and as such has remained a symbol of motherly love. Her place of burial in Beth Lehem is a traditional place of pilgrimage for religious Jews.

THE REBBE OF LIUBAVICH—Liubavich is a Russian village near Mohilev which was, until the Soviet Revolution, the seat of the Shneorson dynasty, leaders of the Habad Chassidim. The Rabbi of Liubavich has settled since in New York and functions as a spiritual guide and teacher. The spiritual life of the Liubavichers centers on the study of the founder's writings (*Tanya*). This group is one of the most active Chassidic groups maintaining schools, *Yeshivot*, and orphanages.

REBBE—(the Yiddish word for rabbi) Term used for Chassidic

leaders and spiritual guides. The *rebbe* or *tzaddik* is not necessarily a halachic scholar or teacher, but guides his followers by virtue of the spiritual power and holiness thought to be inherent in him.

The Rebbe of Gur—Gur is a small town near Warsaw and former seat of the dominant Chassidic dynasty of Poland, that of the Alter family. The dynasty was established by Isaac Meir Alter (1799–1866), a profound Talmudic scholar and author of the *Hiddushei Ha'Rim*. Succeeded by his grandson Judah Aryeh Leib (1864–1948) one of the few Chassidic rabbis to adopt a positive attitude to the rebuilding of Eretz-Israel. He died in Jerusalem and was succeeded by his son Israel.

Reform—Religious trend advocating modification of Orthodox tradition in conformity with the exigencies of contemporary life and thought. The essential difference between Reform and Orthodox Judaism revolves around the authority of the *halacha*; whereas Orthodoxy maintains the Divine authority of the *halacha* in both its biblical and rabbinic expressions, Reform Judaism subjects religious law and customs to the judgment of man. It attempts to differentiate between those elements of the law which are "eternal" and those legal forms and customs which it believes are the product of a particular age.

Satmar—An extreme orthodox segment of Chassidic Jews belonging to the extreme *Neturey Karta* (Guardians of the Walls) community, who in 1935 broke off with *Agudat Israel* party and since have cut all ties with the State of Israel. They reside in Jerusalem and B'ney Brak.

Sephardi—The Jews of the Iberian peninsula and their descendants came to be known as *Sephardi* in distinction to the Jews of the Franco-German tradition who are known as Ashkenazi. The Sephardi Jewry represents a continuation of the Babylonian tradition. After the expulsion of the Jews from Spain in 1492, the word Sephardi was given wider connotation as the Jews from Spain imposed their culture and traditions upon the Jewish communities of North Africa and the Middle East. The word *Sephardi* today is thus frequently used for a Jew belonging to one of the Oriental communities which adopted the *Sephardi* rite whether or not the community is originally of Spanish provenance.

SHAVU'OTH—(Pentacost) The second of the Pilgrim festivals. It occurs on 6 Sivan on the completion of seven full weeks after the "morrow of the Sabbath" when the "sheaf of the wave-offering" of barley was offered up in the Temple. These seven weeks are marked by the Counting of the Omer commemorating the period between the first harvest and the first fruit harvest. Although it has its agricultural significance, it almost exclusively concentrated on the aspect of the festival commemorating the revelation on Mt. Sinai, and in the liturgy it is called "The Season of the Giving of our Torah." Many customs are linked with this festival: *Tikkun Leyl Shavuot* (Reparation of Pentacost Eve)—a whole night prayer established by the Kabbalists in the 16th century. The agricultural aspect is expressed by the custom of bringing an offering of new wheat and fruit to the Temple, a custom that has remained since (but not to the Temple of course). Due to the tradition that King David, Ruth's grandchild, was born and died on Shavuot, The Book of Ruth is read in synagogue. Another ancient custom is to eat dairy food on this festival as a hint to the Torah, which is like "honey and milk under your tongue" (Song of Songs 4:11).

SHMINI A'TZERET—A festive day following immediately the Festival of Tabernacles (Sukkot). In Israel it is the same day of Simchat Torah, a day on which the Torah reading is concluded.

SELIKHOT—(Heb. "penitential prayers," "forgiveness") The name refers to a group of *piyutim*, asking forgiveness for sins. Originally composed for the Day of Atonement and fasting days and later extended to other services.

SHLOM ZACHAR—A gathering with a light refreshment (usually green or chick peas as a fertility symbol) customary in Ashkenazi Jewry at the house of the woman who has given birth to a baby boy. The gathering's purpose is to protect the baby before the day of circumcision.

SANDAK—Person given the honor of holding the child on his knees during the circumcision ceremony.

SE'UDAH SHE'LISHIT—(Heb. "third meal") In Talmudic times it was customary to eat only two meals a day, but since the commandment to honor the Sabbath and call it a delight was interpreted as including food and drink, the rabbis insisted that three meals be taken on the Sabbath (one on Friday evening and the two others during the day). In the course of time a special sanctity became attached to it, particularly under Kabbalistic influence. With the Polish *Chassidim* it became a major feature of religious and social life. Gathering at the table of the *tzaddik* they would spend hours at the sacred meal till late after the end of the Sabbath, listening to their master's mystical discourse and singing hymns or tunes that produced both ecstatic enthusiasm and quiet meditation.

SHTREIMEL—A fur hat worn on Sabbath and religious festivals by Chassidic Jews of Eastern Europe.

SENESH, HANNAH—(1944–1921) A poet and a fighter who joined the *Haganah* and parachuted into Yugoslavia on March 1944, with the intention of organizing the uprising of European Jews against the Nazis. When crossing the border to her native land Hungary, she was captured by the local police, investigated, tortured, and eventually executed on November 7 of that year. Hannah Senesh has become a national symbol of sacrifice and brave devotion.

SEFER HA'BESHT (Ha'Baal Shem-Tov)—The book containing the life, deeds and sayings of the Baal Shem-Tov which was compiled by his pupils. He left after him some 10, 000 followers who constituted the core of the Hasidut Movement.

SIDDUR—The Hebrew Prayer Book; contains the entire liturgy used in the synagogue and at home, including many non-obligatory prayers.

SHEMA ISRAEL—(Heb. "Hear O Israel") The first verse of Deuteronomy 6:4: "Hear, O Israel, the Lord is our God, the Lord is One"). Because of its emphasis on the unity of God, the Shema is considered the Jewish "confession of faith" and a vital part of the liturgy. It is spoken by a Jew on his deathbed, and throughout the centuries Jews undergoing martyrdom have died with the *Shema* on their lips.

SHIVAT TZION—The return to Zion of some of the Babylonian exiles following the declaration of king Cyrus of Persia in the year 538 B.C.

SHLOSHIM—The first 30 days of mourning over one of the seven relatives a Jew is obliged to mourn. Many put up the tombstone on the thirtieth day.

SIMCHAT TORAH—(Heb. "Rejoicing in the Torah") Name given in the Diaspora to the second day of Shemini Atzeret (in Israel it is the day after the Sukkot festival). The reason for this festival is the completion of the reading of Torah (Pentateuch) in the synagogue, a reading that has taken a full year. The celebration of this day is carried out by *Hakafot*—dancing and singing with the Torah books around the *Bimah* (stage) in the synagogue.

SPINOZA, BARUCH—(1632–1677) Dutch Jewish philosopher of a Portuguese Marrano family that had escaped to Amsterdam. Though he had a traditional Jewish education his own philosophic development, greatly influenced by Descartes, led him away from traditional Orthodoxy. His profound and rigorously elaborated pantheistic metaphysics, his radical demand for unfettered freedom of inquiry, and his moral stature have made of him one of the great figures in modern European philosophy. He was one of the pioneers of biblical criticism, which came close to atheism as understood by the authorities at Amsterdam, and led to his excommunication by the Jewish *Sephardi* community in 1656.

SOLOMON—(10th century B.C.) Israelite king; son of David. His great lifework was the construction of the Temple. King Solomon achieved a wide reputation for wisdom and was the subject of many legends in Jewish and Moslem tradition. Several biblical books (Proverbs, Ecclesiastes, Song of Songs) were attributed to him.

SUKKOT—(Tabernacles) The third of the Pilgrim Festivals beginning on Tishri 15 and lasting for seven days, the main aspect of which involves the dwelling in a *Sukkah* (hut) and blessing the four species to be waved in the synagogue during the recitation of the *Hallel* (Praise).

TALIT—Four cornered cloth with fringes used by males as a prayer shawl during the morning (and additional) service; called *talit gadol* (large talit) in order to distinguish it from the *talit katan* (small talit) or *Tzitzit* worn underneath the outer garments. Today many women wear talits.

TALMUD—Name applied to each of two great compilations, distinguished respectively as the Babylonian Talmud (Talmud *Bavli*) and the Palestinian Talmud (Talmud *Yerushalmi*) in which are collected the records of academic discussion and of judicial administration of Jewish Law (*Halacha*). Written by generations of scholars and jurists in several countries during several centuries after 200 C.E. (the approximate date of the completion of the Mishna). Each Talmud consists of the Mishnah together with a Gemara, which is both a commentary on and a supplement to the Mishna. Both Talmuds contain also non-legal or *haggadic* digressions.

TANNA'IM—Tanna (Aram: "one who studies and teaches" especially the Oral Law) Refers to sages whose views are compiled in the Mishnah and Braita. The period of the *Tanna'im* began after Hillel and Shammai and ended with the generation after Rabbi Yehuda Ha'Nasi, 2nd century.

TEFILLIN—Phylacteries worn by Jews during the morning prayer. Two small square leather boxes containing slips inscribed with scriptural passages and traditionally worn on the left arm and on the head by Jewish men during morning weekday prayers.

THE TEMPLE—The House of the Lord, the sanctuary on the Moriyah Mount. in Jerusalem was built by King Solomon in the 10th century B.C. and was the center of the nation's spiritual and religious life. The ritual there included sacrifices. It was destroyed by the Babylonians in 587 B.C. The Shivat Zion people who returned from Babylonia rebuilt it around 515 B.C. but it was destroyed by Titus, the Roman Emperor, on *Av 9* in the year 70 C.E. The day of the destruction has ever since been a day of fasting and prayer. The Temple area is now the site of the Mosque of Omar erected c. 700 C.E.

TISHA B'AV—A fasting day to commemorate the day of the destruction of the First and Second Temples. The fasting customs on this day are even harsher than on Yom Kippur, and the liturgy includes reading the Book of Lamentations while sitting with dim candlelight on the floor or benches as a sign of mourning.

TORAH—Hebrew word referring to the Bible. Its literal meaning is "teaching," "instruction," or "guidance." In rabbinic literature Torah is used in a variety of senses, all based on the general understanding of Torah as the guidance and teaching imparted to Israel by Divine Revelation. Thus it designates the Pentateuch as distinct from the other two main sections of the Hebrew Bible—the Prophets and the Hagiorapha. The comprehensive sense is the Written Law (*Torah She'bikhtav*) and the *Torah She'be'alpeh* (written and oral Torah).

TOSAPHOT—(Heb. "Additions") Beginning as additional interpretations and complements to Rashi's Commentary on the Talmud it grew into a much wider work, much more than an interpretation. The *Tosaphot* were the combined work of French and German Jewish scholars in the 12th and 13th centuries some of whom were offspring of Rashi. The Tosaphot are printed on the outer side of the Talmud page while on the internal side there appears the Rashi commentary.

TZIDUK HA'DIN—(Heb. "justification of the judgment") The acceptance of the justice of the Divine decree especially in the sense of resigned submission to God's justice in the face of a person's death. The term signifies the prayer which is recited at a funeral. Theodicy.

VICHNITZ, THE REBBE OF—The Chassidut of Vichnitz is one of the larger Chassidic communities. Established in Bukovina (Rumania) in the town of Vichnitz by Rabbi Mencahem Mendel.

VIDUI—(Heb. "confession") The admission and acknowledgement of guilt or wrongdoing as a means of expiation and atonement and is one of the three essential elements of true repentance. Confession is the main feature of the Yom Kippur prayers.

USHPIZIN—(Aram. "guests") A legend first mentioned by the *Zohar* to the effect that on each of the seven days of the Festival of Tabernacles (*Sukkot*) one of seven patriarchs or heroes of biblical history (Abraham, Isaac, etc.) is welcomed as a spiritual guest to the Tabernacle. It also became a custom to invite poor students to the tabernacle as symbols for the spiritual visitors.

WALLENBERG, RAOUL—(1906–1947?) A Swedish diplomat who during World War II saved the life of 20,000–100,000 Hungarian Jews by granting them Swedish passports. In 1945 he was captured by the Soviet Army and (probably) sent to a camp in Siberia where died. Yad Va'Shem granted him, after his death, the title of "Righteous Among the Nations" for his good deeds.

WARSAW GHETTO—The Jewish Ghetto, a special urban quarter for the sole residence of Jews. During World War II the Nazis erected new ghettos in Polish and west Russian towns which served as prisons until their transfer to the death camps. The Warsaw Ghetto was famous for its rebellion, headed by Mordekhai Anilevich, against the Nazis, a rebellion that was suppressed and all its participants put to death.

YAD VASHEM—The Holocaust Martyrs' and Heroes' Remembrance Authority, in Jerusalem, Israel.

YESHIVA—The oldest institution for higher learning of the Written and Oral Jewish Law.

YIZKOR—Memorial service in which prayers are offered for the repose of the dead, customary in the Ashkenazi rite on the last days of the three pilgrimage festivals and the Day of Atonement.

YOM KIPPUR—Day of Atonement. The most solemn occasion of the Jewish calendar—the 10th of the month of Tishri. The main features of the day are the "five mortifications": abstention from food, drink, marital intercourse, anointing with oil, wearing leather shoes. During the 25-hour fast, five services of prayer take place, of which the first in the Evening Service is preceded by the recitation of Kol Nidrei. The prayers of the day stress confession of sins and supplications for forgiveness on behalf of the whole congregation of Israel.

ZIONIST MOVEMENT—Movement to secure the return of the Jews to the Land of Israel. Modern political Zionism, as founded by Theodor Herzl at the First Zionist Congress (1897), aimed at a peaceful political solution of the "Jewish Problem."

ZOHAR, THE BOOK OF—A Kabbalistic work composed of several literary units recognized by Kabbalists as the most important of mystical teaching. Contains exchanges and reflections by a group of 2nd-century rabbis and scholars in Palestine led by Simeon bar Yohai. Exposing the esoteric meaning of Scripture. Modern research dates the book to the 13th century (Rabbi Moshe de Leon of Girona Spain).

NOTES

1   Talmud, Tractate Sota, 49a.

2   See Glossary.

3   See Glossary.

4   See also Rabbi Adin Steinsaltz: *A Guide to the Talmud*, Jerusalem, 1984.

5   See also the Book of Nehemiah 9:5.

6   Called also "Kaddish Le'Eilah."

7   Customary to say after the study of the Torah.

8   In this tractate, *Kallah*, the tradition of reciting the *Kaddish* for the elevation of soul of the deceased person is mentioned for the first time.

9   David Biale, *Culture of the Jews* , Ivan Marcus, p. 465.

10 Some add to the prayers *Al Naharot Bavel* (On The Rivers of Babylon) Psalms: 133, *Shirat Ha'azinu* ("Give ear, ye Heavens") Deuteronomy, 32:1–43), *Mizmor le'Asaf* ("Psalm by Asaf") Psalms: 89, and Eleh Ezkera ("These I Shall Remember") from the *Mussaf* of Yom Kippur prayer.

11 Dubnov, *Divrey Yemey Olam* (History of the World), vol. 5, Tel-Aviv, 1958.

12 Dr. Yom-Tov Lewinsky, *Sefer Ha'Moa'dim* (Book of Holidays), vol. 6, Tel-Aviv 1963.

13 The Kabbala is the "best-known and most important Jewish mystical movement." See: G. Wigoder (Ed.), *The Encyclopedia of Jewish Religion*, New York, 1983.

14 Aryeh Morgenstern, *Mystica u-Meshichiut* (Mysticism and Messianism), Jerusalem, 1999.

15 Dr. Zvi Werblowsky, Dr. Geoffrey Wigoder, *The Encyclopedia of the Jewish Religion*, New York, 1988.

16 Finkelstein, *Jewish Self-Government*, New York, 1983.

17 Adam Baruch, *Betom Lev*. And Saul Mayzlish, Interview with Ya'ir Tzaban, MK, Dr. Sneh's disciple.

18 Seven is a basic number in Judaism, beginning with the seven days of creation.

19 A fundamental concept of Judaism is the observance of 613 mitzvot (commandments); however, a non-Jew who is compliant with seven specific mitzvot is considered pious.

20 Harav Israel Meir Lau, *Yahadut Halacha le-Ma'aseh* (The Practice of Judaism), Tel-Aviv, 1998.

21 Akiva Zimmerman, *Beron Yahad* (Together in Singing and Praying), Tel-Aviv, 1988.

22 Yona Silberman, Sha'arey Tefila (Gates of Prayer), Tel-Aviv, 1997. And see Tractate *Brachot* 3a, which tells of Rabbi Yossi who went into one of the ruins of Jerusalem to pray, and was joined there by Eliyahu Hanavi who told him he should have prayed on the road rather then enter the ruin. Thereupon Rabbi Yossi responded that he feared he could be interrupted by wayfarers. Eliyahu then advised him to recite a shortened version of the prayer. Rabbi Yossi replied that during his prayer he heard an echo like a dove cooing and saying: Woe unto the sons for whose sins I have destroyed my dwelling and burnt down my Temple and exiled them among the nations. To that Eliyahu replied: Not only this single hour of prayer refers to this, but at all three prayers each day do so, and also at the prayers the people of Israel recite when they go into their synagogues and Batey-Midrash, "Yehe Shmei Rabba Mevorach" (Let the name of God be blessed) The Lord then nods his head and says: Happy is the king who is thus praised in his home, how did the father exile his sons and woe unto these sons who were banished from their father's table.

23 Harav Adin Steinsaltz, *Ha'Siddur ve'Hatefila* (The Siddur and the Prayer), Jerusalem, 1996.

24 See also "*Zoharim*," Tel Aviv, 1963.

25 Shmuel Yosef Agnon, "*Samuch Ve-Nir'eh*" (Close and Visible) Collected works, Volume 3, p. 288, Jerusalem, 1964.

26 See also Rabbi Israel Hess, *Emunot* (Beliefs) (according to Orot Hateshuva by Avraham Itzhak Hacohen Kook), Ra'anana, 1986.

27 See also Harav Prof. Simcha Bunim Urbach, *Amudey Hamakhshava ha-Israelit* (Pillars of Israeli Thought), Volume I, Part 2, Jerusalem, 1972.

28 Levin (Ed.), *Eleh Maias'ey: Reshimat Masa Ha'Rabanim Kook Ve'Sonnenfeld* (The Journey of the Rabbis Kook and Sonnenfeld), Netanya, 2001. Shmuel Hacohen-Avidor, *Ha'Ish Neged Hazerem* (The Man Against the Current), Jerusalem, 1973.

29 Levin (Ed.), *Eleh Maias'ey : Reshimat Masa Ha'Rabanim Kook Ve'Sonnenfeld* (The Journey of the Rabbis Kook and Sonnenfeld), Netanya, 2001. Shmuel Hacohen-Avidor, *Ha-Ish Neged Hazerem* (The Man Against the Current), Jerusalem, 1973.

30 Yom-Tov Lewinsky, *Sefer Ha'Mo'adim—Seder Ta'aniyot. Asara Be'Tevet,* Tel-Aviv, 1974.

31 Harav Dr. Yitzhak Alfassi, *Hassidut* (Hassidism), Tel-Aviv, 1983.

32 Bromberg, *Hassidut Berdichev—Rabbi Levi Yitzhak,* Tel-Aviv, 1971.

33 Ezra Hartman, *Dor Le'Dor Yabi'a Omer* (From Generation to Generation), Petach-Tiqva, 1993.

34 Menachem Michelson, *Kivrey Zadikim* (Tombs of the Righteous), Tel Aviv, 1999.

35 Saul Mayzlish is a direct descendant of the Rama, a distinguished rabbi who made editorial comments on the *Shulchan Aruch* written by Rabbi Joseph Karo, a sefardic scholar, the legal code for Jewish life. The Rama's comments established the Shulchan Aruch, acceptable to Ashkenazi Jews ever since the 16th century.

36 Pnina Miller, *Harav Sheli* (My Rabbi), Tel-Aviv, 1986.

37 The founder of Chassidism in the 17th century.

38 An interview with Shlomo Ness, Galey Tzahal Radio, Tel-Aviv, 2004.

39 An acronym for Rabbi Luria Ashkenazi whose mystical concepts and Kabbalistic teachings became the foundation of mystical and kabbalistic thought for generations to come. See also Glossary.

40 Harav Shmuel Avidor Hacohen, *Machanayim,* vol. 3, issue 3a, Tel Aviv, 1958.

41 Saul Mayzlish, *Eropa shel Ya'hadut* (Europe of Judaism), Tel-Aviv, 1985.

42 The cantillation of the *Kaddish* is usually a fixed traditional tune; some of its motifs were later developed by famous composers such as Ravel, Bloch, and Bernstein.

43 Saul Mayzlish, see note 35 above.

44 See also Elenbogen-Y. Heinemann, *Ha'tfila Be'Israel Be'Hitpatchuta Ha'historit* (The Prayer in Israel and its Historical Development), Jerusalem, 1988. Words from ancient Jewish prayers, for instance, the Thanksgiving for the Rain (Talmud Yerushalmi, Ta'anit 1:3) were included in the *Kaddish.* How ironic that the Germans did not know that the prayer to Jesus "Our Father Who Art in Heaven" (Matthew 6:9–10) recalls in its beginning some of the Kaddish words.

45 Harav Eli Roth, *Kerem D'Yavneh* (Yavneh's Vinyard), Jerusalem, 1997.

46 Among the Midrashim of Redemption and the Coming of the Messiah: *Ta'anit* 5a ("I shall come into Heavenly Jerusalem until I shall come into Earthly Jerusalem") (*Psikta Rabati* 36 and *Tractate Sanhedrin* 98b).

47 Part of the mystery is linked with the name *Kaddish*, which is not to be found in the Talmud and Midrashim, and is mentioned for the first time after the conclusion of the Talmud, during the period of Rabanan Sevora'i (Aramaic: Explaining Rabbis) the sages whose role was to explain and who acted in Babylon between the year 500 until the year 600, the beginning of the Geo'nim period.

48 See also David Margalit, *Tefilat HaKaddish, Mekoroteiha ve-Nusacha'oteiha* ("The Kaddish Prayer—Sources and Versions"), Jerusalem, 1986.

49 Pninah Miller, op. cit.

50 Saul Mayzlish, *Brith Milah* (Circumcision) from the trilogy *Ad 120*, Tel-Aviv 1985.

51 Saul Mayzlish, *Ani Ma'amin-Al Emunot Tefelot* (I Believe: On Superstitions), Tel-Aviv, 1998.

52 Rabbi Ya'akov ben Rabbi Moshe Halevi Mulin (14th C. acronym—Maharil) of Mainz, thinks that the *Kaddish Yatom* was especially arranged for children since they could not be members of a *minyan* and were upset by this. The *Kaddish* prayer is the only one permitted for children and they are obliged to recite it; this is why it is so important.

53 David Shapira, *Mekhkarim shel Minhagey Avelut* (Studies of Mourning Customs), Jerusalem, 1997.

54 *Yahadut* (Judaism], Tel-Aviv, 1978, p. 468. As well as other *Machazorim* (Prayer Books). See also Miller Rochelle, *Woman and Kaddish, Reflection of Responsa*, and David Telzner, *The Paean of Redemption-on the Meaning of the Kaddish*, New York, 1989.

55 Saul Mayzlish, *Ein Shalem MiLev Shavur* (Nothing Is as Whole as a Broken Heart), Tel-Aviv, 1989.

56 See also Adam Baruch, *Seder Yom* (Agenda), Jerusalem, 2001.

57 An interview with Yitzhak Sonnenshein, the Israeli Television. Jeusalem, 1999.

58 See also the entry "Avelut" (Mourning) in *The Hebrew Encyclopedia* (Encyclopedia Ivrit), vol. 1. p. 160.

59 Saul Mayzlish, *Eropa shel Yahadut*, op. cit.

60 Shlomo Zalman Ariel, *Encyclopedia Meir Nativ*, Tel-Aviv, 1971.

61 There were also other various customs of mourning; for example, the custom of throwing sand and herbs behind one's back when returning from the

cemetery. The Jews were suspected of casting a spell on their gentile neighbors by doing so.

62 Saul Mayzlish, *Eropa shel Yahadut*.

63 Harav Y. Yakobson, *Netiv Binah (Way of Wisdom)*, Tel-Aviv, 1967.

64 See also David Pri-Chen, *Tefilat Ha'Kaddish* (The Kaddish Prayer), Jerusalem, 1989.

65 See also Yehuda David Eisenstein, *Encyclopedia Otzar Israel* (Treasure of Israel), 2, New York, 1934.

66 Y. Baer, *Toldot Ha'Yehudim Bi'Sfarad Ha'Notzrit* (The History of the Jews in Christian Spain), Jerusalem, 1974.

67 Saul Mayzlish, *Ein Shalem Mi'Lev Shavur*, Tel-Aviv, 1982.

68 See also the article "Avelut" (Mourning) in *The Hebrew Encyclopedia*, Tel -Aviv, 1965, vol. I, p. 158.

69 *The Hebrew Encyclopedia*, the entry "Mas'ey Hatzlav" (the Crusades), vol. 19.

70 The introduction of the *Kaddish* to the community was slow. Even when it was initially performed in the elite's funerals, it was still a direct continuation of the custom to recite the *Kaddish* after studies shifted to the burial rites of *Gedoley Israel* (The Great Rabbis of Israel). Indeed, the *Kaddish* differs from the regular prayers in its style and language (Aramaic); it addresses God indirectly (in the third person), such as "Kudsha brich hu" (The Sacred {God} be Blessed), or "Avuhun di Bi'Shmei" (Our Father in Heaven). In the first passage it even speaks just of "his great name." At the end of every passage the public is addressed by "*ve-imru Amen*." All these traits derive directly from the original role of the *Kaddish*: an ending of a public sermon, usually recited in Aramaic. The speaker refers to God indirectly, using three attributes. The messianic tone, too, links with endings of sermons which were often taken from the Consolation prophesies. See *The Hebrew Encyclopedia*, vol. 9, p. 156.

71 Dr. Yom-Tov Lewinsky, op. cit. vol 8. *Yom Mo'ed Ve'Zikaron* (A Day of Festival and Memory), Tel-Aviv, 1964.

72 See "Mi Yiten Roshi Mayim" ("Who Will Render my Head Water?") by Klonimos ben Rabbi Yehuda Shapira, 12th C. Extract from a lamentation for Tisha B'Av over the Crusades massacres, after the custom of Ashkenaz and Poland.

73 Rabbi Yosef Hacohen, *Divrey Hayamim Le'malchei Zorfat U'Malchey Otman Hatogar* (The History of the Kings of France and Turkey), 1554, Venice.

74 Conservative and Reform Judaism include women in the *minyan*.

75 See also Hillel Ben-Yaakov, *Emuney Shlomei Israel*, from *Selikha le Mussaf Yom Ha'Kippurim* (Forgiveness to the Supplement of the Day of Atonement).

76 See Death on *Kiddush Hashem* (martyrdom) in York, England 1190, according

to *Sefer Ha'dma'ot* (the Book of Tears), Sh. Bernfeld, part 1 and *Kinat Ha'kdoshim al Ha'shmad* (The Lament of the Holy on the Forced Conversion) during *Khol Ha'Mo'ed, Colonia* (Cologne, Germany), a lament recited on the first Sabbath after Pesach customary in Poland and was written by Rabbi Yitzhak Ben Shalom.

77 See Rabbi Shlomo de Virga, *Gzerot Ha'me'tzora'im ve Ha'mavet-Ha'shachor* (The Lepers' Decrees and the Black Death), from *Shevet Yehuda* 43, and also S. Baron, *Melo Ha'Ribonut Ha'Apostolit Ve'Shi'abud Ha'Yehudim* (The Entire Apostolic Sovereignty and the Subjection of the Jews), *Sefer Ha'Yovel le Yitzhak Baer* (Jubilee Volume presented to Yitzhak Baer).

78 Chaim H. Ben-Sasson, "Mekoma shel Ha'Kehila-Ir, Kiddush Ha'Shem u-Martyrium," *Ha'ir Ve'Hakehila* ("The Place of the Community-Town, Kiddush HaShem and Martyrdom"). And A. D. Haberman, *Sefer G'zerot Ashkenaz Ve'-Zorfat* (The Book of Decrees {of punishment or prohibition} on Germany and France) and Y. Baer, *Gzerot Tatnu. Sefer Asaf*, Jerusalem, 1953.

79 There was a problematic of *Chukot Ha'goyim* (The Laws of the Gentiles) and the adoption of their customs. See debate on the entry "Chukot Ha'goyim" in *The Talmudic Encyclopedia*, ch. 17. The basis of the problematic is the verse "*Lo Tilmad La'asot Ke'Toa'vot Ha'Goyim Ha'hem*" (You shall not learn to do the gentiles' abominations, Deuteronomy 18:9; as well as "*Lo Titgodedu*" (You must not cluster in the nude) (Deuteronomy 14:1; and also Tur, Yore De'a, in 310, who discusses the prohibition to imitate the gentiles by building theaters and circuses, or emulating their dress, haircut, etc. However, in the issue of prayer there is no "*To'e'vot Ha'goyim*" (gentiles' abominations) and therefore emulating their traits and rituals is permitted.

80 Ch. H. Ben-Sasson (Ed.), *Toldot Am Israel Ve'Hashilton Ha'Roma'I* (The History of the People of Israel and the Roman Rule), Jerusalem, 1982.

81 Yom-Tov Lewinksy, op. cit., Tel Aviv, 1965.

82 *Ibid.* See also Yemey Mo'ed ve-Khorban (Holidays and Memorial Days of Destruction).

83 See also *Sefer Shiboley Haleket, Din Arba'a Ha'tzomot* (The Law of the Four Fasts), 263, Jerusalem. As well as the lamentation for Tish'a B'Av on the burning of the Talmud in Paris, *Sha'ali Srufa Ba'esh* (Beg, You Burnt by Fire) by the Maharam (Rabbi Meir) of Rothenburg, Germany.

84 *Encyclopedia Klalit*, vol. 8, "the Ghetto," Tel-Aviv, 1966.

85 The concept of the ghetto being the arena of persecution and torture was epitomized in the Ghetto of Strasbourg. On February 14th, 1349, on St. Valentine's Day, the gentiles, believing that the Jews intended to blow the shofar to signal the enemy to enter the town, sealed the ghetto and drove out all the

Jews to the cemetery where they burned them alive—more than 2,000 people! For 200 years Jews were forbidden to live in the city.

86 The Hamisha-Assar Fasting Day (The 15th Day Fast) on the month of Kislev and Yizkor to the Carpantus community who in the year 1511 were saved from the mob riots.

87 A blood libel took place in Trent, Italy, in 1475. The Jews were accused of concealing a two-year-old child by the name of Simon. Confessions were extracted by torture and all the accused were executed. The baby Simon was then declared a Saint by the Catholic Church, but in 1965 his sainthood was annulled. (Ch. Ben-Sasson, *Toldot Am Israel*, p. 188).

88 Blood libel, *Min-Ha'massad Encyclopedia* (From the Foundation), Tel-Aviv, 1987.

89 The same in England, 1144; in Blois, France, the local Jews were burned in 1171 following a blood libel. The same in Pulda, Germany, where in 1348 the Jews were accused of stealing and stabbing the Host, which symbolizes the body of Christ. These Christians believed that the Host bled when stabbed, like a wound in the flesh. 154 Blood Libels were counted, including 45 in Germany, 20 in Poland, 16 in Austria, 14 in Romania, 12 in Italy, 9 in Russia and 7 in France. In 1840 the Jews of Damascus were accused of murdering a monk named Adolph Cremier. Only with the help of Moshe Montefiore was the libel exposed, and the Turkish authorities produced a "firman" for the protection of the Jews. In Hungary, in the town of Tisa-Aslar, in the year 1882–1883 a blood libel was devised against the Jews.

90 The autonomy of the Jewish leadership during and after the Black Plague once more increased the rabbis' authority. The rabbis introduced and established the *Kaddish* recital at the massive funerals resulting from the Plague. They even won the title of "leaders." The title of *Rosh Ha'galut* (Exilarch) too was back in use. Rabbi Israel Iserles attacked their inclination to see themselves as the "Lords of the Place" (Mara D'atra) not letting any other Talmid Chacham (Scholar) serve in their region . In Ashkenaz (Germany) the rabbinical leadership was very firm about their right of authority and rule over their public. See Ch. H. Ben-Sasson, op.cit.

91 *Al Takanot Ha'Kehilot Bi'Sfarad* (On the Instructions of the Communities in Spain), *Hatashbetz*, part 3, sign 13, Jerusalem, 1959.

92 Cadiz in Spain was the first to receive the Marranos who arrived there after the persecutions in 1391. From there the expelled Jews left for the ports of North Africa.

93 Auto-da-fe, the literal meaning of this horribly cruel practice is "act of faith." By blaming people for heresy and burning them alive at the stake, the Church aimed to reinforce the Catholic faith among the common people.

The Church thus executed around 30,000 Jews in its effort to persuade them to convert to Christianity. It is possible that some of the persecutions and killings were aimed at abolishing certain customs copied from the Christians such as the prayer recited at the funeral. See the *Min Ha'massad Encyclopedia*, p. 15.

94 In the *Selichot* recited in the *Yamim Nora'im* (High Holidays) and on public fasts there exist, too, the goal to unite the community through the prayers recited in a fixed format. The *Selichot* (prayers begging forgiveness) were created by the Ge'onim and some of the greater poets like Rabbi Shlomo Ibn Gabirol, Rabbi Yehuda Halevi, and Rabbi Moshe Ibn Ezra. As with the *Kaddish* prayer, a special folklore was created around them in the Diaspora. Believers used to get up before the crack of dawn to recite them and the synagogue's *Shamash* (sexton) would walk around knocking on people's windows to urge them to get up and pray. It is still the custom to this day in some of the Oriental Jewish communities.

95 The prayer for remembrance and the elevation of souls of the dead. Though the prayer— *Yizkor Elokim et Nishmat . . .* ("God shall Remember the Soul of . . .")—is called *Yizkor* (Rememberance)—is not explicit in the words of Chazal or the Ge'onim, it was observed in all the Jewish communities, and was part of the strictly observed custom of giving charity as part of the loved one's soul elevation. See *Min Ha'massad Encyclopedia*, p. 77.

96 *Chevra Kaddisha*, see Glossary

97 Beyt Hamidrash is described in the Agadda literature which told of Shem and Ever (Genesis) who were the first to establish a Beyt Midrash where the Founders of the Nation studied.

98 Beyt Din is an institution originating in the Torah: "*Shoftim ve-Shotrim Titen Lecha Bechol She'areicha*" ("Judges and Officers shalt thou make thee in all thy gates, Deuteronomy 16:18). *Beyt Ha'Din Ha'Gadol* (The Great Court) in Jerusalem, the "*Sanhedrin Gedola*" (The Great Sanehdrin), had 71 Dayanim (judges) and the "Sanhedrin Ketana"23. In Bavel there were *Batey Din* next to the community leaders and the Geonim. The Jews in the Diaspora preferred to be judged by their own court (*Beyt Din*) rather than by the gentile courts, and thus they strengthened its autonomy. *Ibid.*, p. 38.

99 *Encyclopedia Klalit*, vol. 3.

100 Eliezer Steinman, *Be'er Ha'talmud* (The Well of the Talmud), Tel-Aviv, 1962.

101 See also Dubnov S., op. cit., vol 7, Tel-Aviv, 1963, "The Messianic Movement Among the Jews."

102 *Ibid.*, p. 121.

103 See also *Encyclopedia Klalit*, vol. 1, "Avelut" (Mourning), vol. 1, Tel-Aviv, 1965.

104 Eliezer Steinman, op. cit., Tel-Aviv, 1981.

105 See more at length: Avraham Yehoshua Heshel, *Torah min Ha'Shamayim Be'Aspaklariat Ha'Dorot* (Torah from Heaven as Reflected in the Mirror of the Generations), Tel-Aviv, 1963.

106 *Ibid.*, p. 20.

107 One very interesting phenomenon of the author's "voyage" through *Kaddish* was that he met individuals who were quite dubious at the outset to saying *Kaddish* (usually 3 times a day for 11 months). Ironically when the year was up, I found many of these individuals had trouble detoxifying from the process. The author felt and was told that while they were in the process they felt healing and camaraderie with the others saying *Kaddish* and a genuine internal spiritual experience. They seemed a bit lost on the day they fulfilled their commitment. Why? Because they had become members of a community with a highly structured ritual commitment. The individual now had to make a decision to stay with the community which rabbinical Judaism always encourages. Judaism precludes excessive mourning. The Jewish mourning process encourages a gradual reentry into society and community after strict structural periods of mourning. Once again we see that rabbinical Judaism basically aims to constitute and regulate the community.

108 The *minyan* principle of ten people for prayer contains also the element of mutual guarantee.

109 They continued to reinforce the special status of the scholars which was formed into an elite in the Yeshivot of Babylon, remaining till the end of the Ge'onim period (mid 10th C.) and have become the leadership and creators of the Jewish spiritual life and the mainstay of the Jewish community. See Ben-Sasson, op. cit.

INDEX

Ruth L. Rockwood Memorial Library
The Public Library of Livingston

10 ROBERT H. HARP DRIVE • LIVINGSTON, NEW JERSEY 07039

GAYLORD RG